ST(P) Handbooks for Further Education

# PREPARING AND USING CONSTRUCTED-ANSWER QUESTIONS

*ST(P) Handbooks for Further Education* will be an open-ended series on topics of interest for all concerned with teaching and administration in post-secondary education. *Preparing and Using Constructed-answer Questions* is the second of three titles on assessment being written by Christine Ward formerly of the City & Guilds of London Institute. The two other titles are:

*Designing a Scheme of Assessment*

*Preparing and Using Objective Questions*

ST(P) Handbooks for Further Education

# Preparing and Using Constructed-answer Questions

CHRISTINE WARD

Stanley Thornes (Publishers) Ltd

First published in 1981 by Stanley Thornes (Publishers) Ltd.,
Educa House, Old Station Drive, off Leckhampton Road,
CHELTENHAM, GL53 ODN

British Library Cataloguing in Publication Data

Ward, Christine
Preparing and using constructed-answer questions.
(Handbooks for further education series; 2).
1. Universities and colleges — Examinations
2. Adult education
3. Vocational education
I. Title II. Series
374 LC5225.E/

ISBN 0-85950-433-6

Typesetting by Permanent Typesetting & Printing Co. Ltd., Hong Kong
Printed in Great Britain by Ebenezer Baylis & Son Ltd., Worcester

# Contents

# Foreword

In recent years further education has seen a trend away from centrally set national examinations towards examinations and assessments set by the college and validated by the award-making body (Technician Education Council, Business Education Council, etc.). More lecturers in further education are now being required to set examinations and in-course tests for outside validation, as well as internal examinations. Some groups of colleges have joint schemes, with jointly set examinations and tests, and there is therefore an increased need for moderation of question papers and coordination of marking.

My aim in this book is to provide help and guidance for all those in colleges who are concerned with the planning, setting, moderating, marking and reviewing of constructed-answer (i.e. non-objective) examinations and tests, as well as for assessors, moderators, external examiners and staff working for the award-making bodies.

This book is intended to help you, the reader, to make your examinations more valid (i.e. appropriate) and more reliable, by demonstrating the principles and techniques of 'good' examining. It cannot supply the knowledge of the individual subject, course and students which are also necessary to the production of a good examination and which you, the subject expert, must therefore supply. I have, however, included examples of questions and marking schemes drawn from a wide range of subjects in order to illustrate the points I make.

The planning, production, marking and analysis of an examination take place over a long period of time, usually with a gap of one or two years between planning and production, and a gap of several months between production and marking. The book is divided into separate parts, each relevant to one of these stages, so that, for example, Part II can be consulted when the examination is being planned and Part III when it is being written and moderated. You are, however, urged to read Part I first, as this contains a discussion of the reasons for good practice which underlies all the rest of the book — it is not designed as an 'optional extra' but as an essential part of the argument.

Part V of the book is concerned with the analysis and review of the examination and with question banking; it considers the interpretation of the various statistical information which can be obtained for an examination. The calculations involved are explained, with worked examples, in the Appendices.

Although the book has been written mainly with the end-of-course examination in mind, most of what is said is equally applicable to constructed-answer tests set during the course.

The chapters on moderating and on coordination of marking are particularly relevant to situations where two or more colleges share a joint syllabus and examination.

Each chapter is followed by a section headed 'Application' which contains questions or suggestions for investigations. These are intended to help you to apply the contents of the chapter to a constructed-answer paper with which you are personally concerned — for example, a paper which you yourself set or moderate.

I would like to acknowledge how much I learned from the staff, examiners and committee members under whom, and with whom I worked at City & Guilds.

I am grateful to City & Guilds of London Institute for permission to reproduce the following examples, although it should be noted that the Institute is not responsible for the accuracy of any solutions and marking schemes given: Examples 1.1, 1.2, 1.3, 1.4, 1.5, 1.6, 1.7, 1.9, 1.10, 1.11, 1.13, 1.14, 1.15, 1.16, 1.17, 2.1, 2.2, 2.3, 2.4, 2.5, 2.7, 3.1, 3.3, 3.6, 3.7, 3.9, 3.11, 3.12, 3.14, 3.16, 4.1, 4.2, 4.3, 4.5, 4.6, 5.1, 5.2, 5.3, 5.4, 6.1, 6.2, 6.3, 6.5, 6.6, 6.7, 6.8, 6.9, 6.10, 6.11, 6.12, 6.14, 6.15, 6.16, 6.18, 6.19, 6.20, 6.21, 6.22, 6.23, 6.24, 6.25, 6.26, 6.27, 6.28, 6.30, 6.31, 6.32, 6.35, 6.36, 7.2, 7.3, 7.4, 7.5, 7.6, 8.1, 8.2, 8.3, 8.4, 8.5, 8.6, 8.7, 8.8, 8.10, 8.11, 8.13, 8.14, 8.15, 8.16, 8.17, 8.18, 8.19, 9.3, 12.2, 12.3, 16.2, 16.4, 17.1.

I am also grateful to the following organisations for permission to reproduce material:

The Business Educational Council for Examples 1.8 and 3.5; the Union of Educational Institutions for Examples 2.6, 3.15 and 9.1; the Scottish Business Education Council for Examples 3.4 and 9.2.

I would like to thank Miss Dorothy Francis for help with Example 12.1 and Mr Arthur Gee for help with Examples 3.10 and 8.17.

I would like to thank John Twining for his help and constructive comments during the writing of the book and Miss 'Blue' Stevens for retyping parts of the manuscript.

Finally I should like to thank my husband, Arthur, for his encouragement, for much advice, comment and constructive criticism and for taking a share of domestic and child-minding chores in order to give me time to write.

*London* *C. Ward*

PART I

# The Use of Constructed-answer Questions

The three chapters in this part lay the foundations of the rest of the book. Chapter 1 looks at the definition of constructed-answer questions and at the different types which are used. Chapter 2 considers the reasons for using constructed-answer questions and in particular the circumstances in which they are to be preferred to the normally more reliable objective questions. Chapter 3 discusses the measures which may be taken to improve constructed-answer questions so as to bring them closer to the standards of reliability set by objective questions and also so as to make them more valid, i.e. appropriate.

The considerations discussed in Chapter 3 underlie the 'good practice' which is recommended in the chapters which follow. Consequently this part of the book is intended, not as an 'optional extra', but as essential to the appreciation of the rest of the book.

# 1

# What are Constructed-answer Questions?

## Definition

Constructed-answer questions are any examination or test questions for which the student has to compose his own answer, in writing, drawing or by calculation. They contrast, therefore, with objective questions (the best known of which are multiple-choice) for which the student has only to select the correct answer from a number of given alternatives. Constructed-answer questions may be used both in end-of-course or end-of-unit examinations and in in-course tests ('phased' written tests).

## Types of Constructed-answer Question

Constructed-answer questions may be divided into three main types: *short-answer*, *structured* and *unstructured*. The three types merge into one another but in general the following descriptions apply.

A *short-answer* question is one which can be answered within five minutes, sometimes much less. The length of answer required may vary from a single word, as in Example 1.1, to a few lines, as in Example 1.2

*A structured* question requires a longer time, usually 20—30 minutes per

---

### EXAMPLES

**1.1** *Electrical Technicians*

Of what material is the bit of an electric soldering iron usually made?

**1.2** *Chemical Technicians*

Explain why the pressure of an ideal gas is proportional to the concentration of the gas.

question. The distinguishing feature of a structured question is that it is subdivided in such a way that the student is directed in some detail to the structure of the answer required and the nature of the points to be included. The parts of the question should be closely related and may deal with different aspects of a given practical situation, as in Example 1.3. The term 'structured question' is sometimes applied inappropriately to a question

## EXAMPLE

### 1.3 *Mechanical Engineering Technicians*

The piston in the figure below is to be made from phosphor-bronze, and operates freely in a cylinder bored in a cast iron block.

(a) What are the advantages of using phosphor-bronze for this part?

(b) In what form of supply would the bronze be received?

(c) Set out a sequence of operations for the production of the piston by machining.

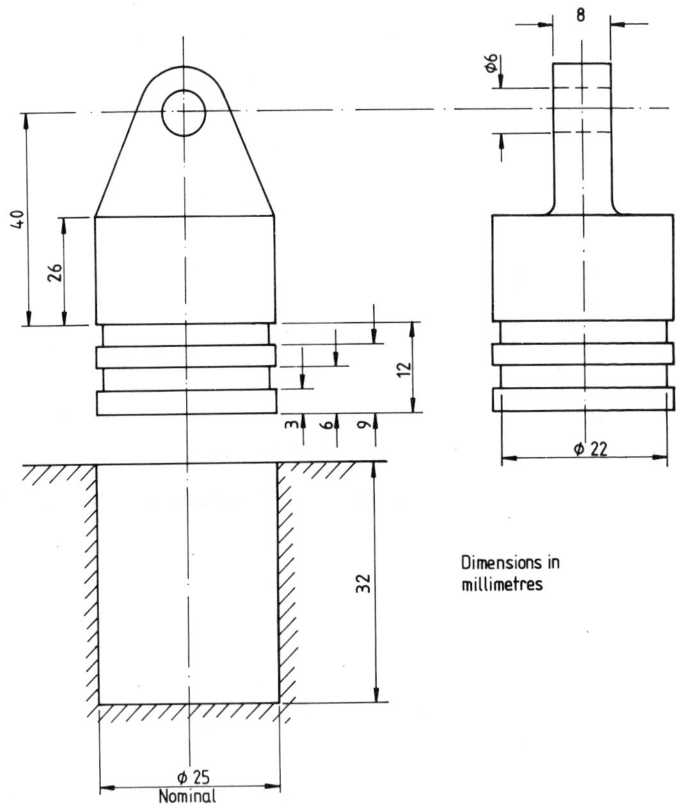

whose parts are only very loosely related, so that it bears more resemblance to a collection of short-answer questions.

An *unstructured* question gives only the minimum of guidance to the student as to what is expected and he or she must decide what points are relevant to the question and how the material is to be organised. The most common type of unstructured question is the essay question, as in Example 1.4.

## EXAMPLES

**1.4** *National Distribution Certificate*

Write an article for a magazine on *one* of the following topics:

(a) Every day is different,

(b) In at the deep end.

(c) Behind the scenes.

(d) People at work.

Indicate the name of the magazine at the end of the article

**1.5** *Electrical Craft*

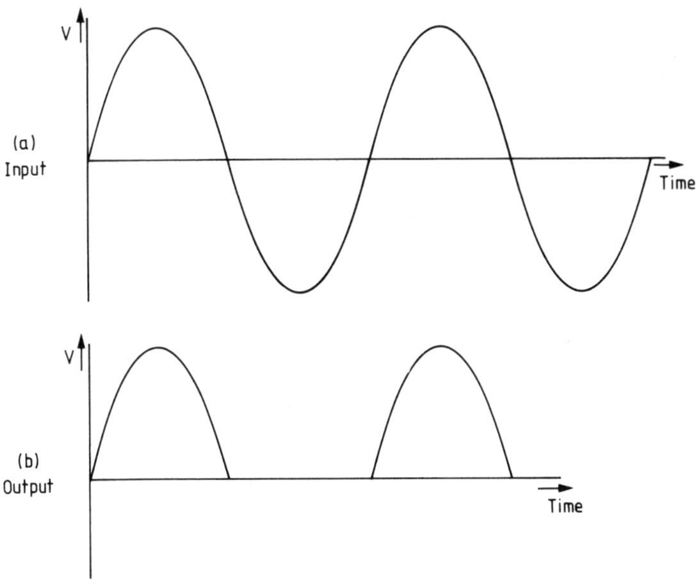


Draw a simple diagram of a circuit which would produce the output (b) from the input (a) shown above.

## Forms of Answer

*Written* answers have been required by all the examples given so far, but constructed-answer questions may require answers in other forms.

*Drawing and sketching* are often required, either to test the student's ability in drawing and sketching or as a medium for showing his technical understanding. Example 1.5 is a short-answer sketching question, designed mainly to assess the student's technical knowledge and capable of being answered in a short time. Example 1.6 is a structured drawing question; the student is told what aspects of the plant his answer is to show. Example 1.7 is an unstructured drawing question.

*Calculations* and *graphical* work may be required in answer to constructed-answer questions. Example 1.8 shows a short-answer calculation question. Examples 1.9 and 1.10 show two ways in which a short-answer question may test knowledge of graphs. Example 1.11 is a structured question involving

---

### EXAMPLES

**1.6** *Technical Graphics, Botanical Illustration*

Make an illustration in pencil of the specimen provided, to present a well-balanced arrangement on a sheet of A4 paper. The illustration must show clearly the botanical character of the specimen and consist of separate drawings as indicated below. Each drawing may be to any suitable scale. The individual scale of each drawing must be clearly stated and the name of the plant must be included as part of the layout.

COLUMBINE (*Aquilegia hybrida*)

(i) growth habit of the plant,

(ii) leaf structure and insertion,

(iii) part of the stem with leaves, buds and flowers,

(iv) single flower, whole and in its separate parts in dissection.

**1.7** *General Course in Construction, Drawing*

A lean-to roof abuts a 275 mm brick cavity wall.
Draw a vertical section through the upper part of the 100 mm by 50 mm timber rafter, felt, battened and plain tiled roof at the junction with the main wall to show all construction.
Fully annotate your drawing.
Scale 1 to 10.

**1.8** *Business Calculations*

Five-litre cans of golden syrup cost a grocer £2.50 a can and he sells them for £4.25. What percentage profit does he make calculated on the selling price?

**1.9** *Footware Manufacture Technicians*

Sketch a graph to show how the strength of an adhesive bond develops from the time of bonding until 24 hours have elapsed.

## EXAMPLES

### 1.10 *Electrical Craft Studies*

The figure below shows two sinusoidal waveforms of the same amplitude but different frequency. On the same axes sketch the waveform of the two voltages added together.

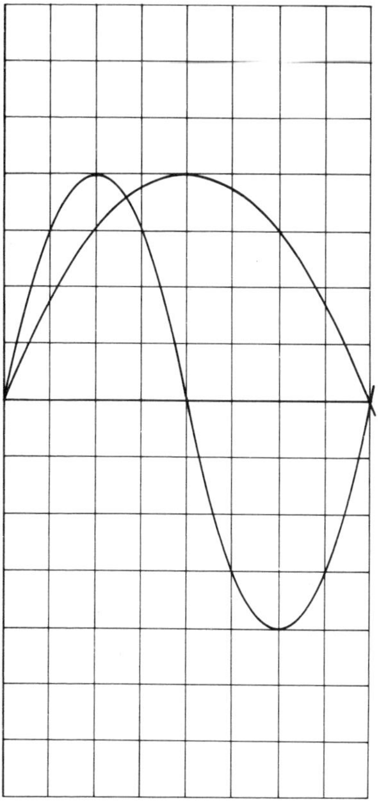

### 1.11 *Electrical Technicians*

(a) Compile a table to show the values of $y_1 = 9 + 10x - 4x^2$ at unit intervals between $x = -1$ and $x = 4$. (6 marks)

(b) On the same axes, between $x = -1$ and $x = 4$, plot accurately the graphs of

(i) $y_1 = 9 + 10x - 4x^2$

(ii) $y_2 = 5 - 3x$ (8 marks)

(c) From the graphs drawn in (b), determine

(i) the solution of the equation $9 + 10x - 4x^2 = 0$

(ii) the range of values of $x$ for which $y_1 > y_2$ (4 marks)

(d) Find the equation whose roots are given by the points of intersection of $y_1 = 9 + 10x - 4x^2$ and $y_2 = 5 - 3x$. (2 marks)

both calculations and graphs; part of the same information could be assessed by an unstructured question, as in Example 1.12

A *combination* of forms of answer may be required. A structured question may require a combination of written answer and drawing or of sketching and calculations.

An unstructured question may also be intended to elicit a combination of different forms of answer, but unless the question specifically states what is expected, the examiner may not get the form of answer intended. For example, the question shown as Example 1.12 could be written simply as 'Solve the equation $9 + 10x - 4x^2 = 0$', but in that case the student would not be limited to a graphical solution.

## Type of Ability Tested

Examination questions make different demands upon the student's ability and level of knowledge; some demand only the recall of memorised information, others require its understanding or its use in a given situation. The best known scheme for classifying the levels of ability required to answer examination questions is B.S. Bloom's *Taxonomy of Educational Objectives* (London: Longmans, 1956). Bloom arranged the abilities in a hierarchy consisting of knowledge, comprehension, application, analysis, synthesis and evaluation; to avoid possible confusion over 'knowledge', the term 'recall of facts' will be used instead in this book, for the lowest category. Because the classification is a hierarchy, each ability must include, in some measure, those preceding it. For example, comprehension is only possible if there is also some recall and a question testing application of facts also requires some degree of recall and understanding. In general, however, the following definitions apply.

*Recall of facts* involves only the reproduction of memorised information. It may be tested by short-answer questions, like Example 1.1 and Example 1.13,

---

### EXAMPLES

**1.12** *Electrical Technicians*

Solve graphically the equation $9 + 10x - 4x^2 = 0$.

**1.13** *Meat Industry Craft Certificate*

Give a list of ingredients necessary for making 20 lb of meat into sausages, complying with legal requirements.

or by structured questions such as part (b) of Example 1.3. Unstructured questions are not usually a suitable method of testing recall, since the small amount of guidance given to the student makes it difficult to ensure that he or she includes the facts expected by the examiner; if he omits a particular piece of information it is impossible to be sure whether this is because he does not know it or because he does not consider it relevant.

'Recall of facts' is equivalent to the Technician Education Council's category 'Information'.

*Comprehension* concerns the understanding of what has been learnt. It may be tested by short-answer questions, as in Examples 1.2 and 1.14, or by structured questions, as in part (a) of Example 1.3. Unstructured questions, are not usually the best method of testing comprehension, although Example 1.7 would certainly require an understanding of building methods.

*Application* concerns the student's ability to use his knowledge in situations which are new to him, thus requiring more than mere recall or even comprehension. Application may be tested by short-answer questions, such as Examples 1.8, 1.10 and 1.15, but is often more easily assessed in the course of a structured question, as in part (c) of Example 1.3. Application would be needed in order to answer Example 1.7, but an essay question such as Example 1.4 could be answered without the student giving any indication of his ability to apply his knowledge to given situations.

In question classification, any analysis, synthesis and evaluation required are often classed with application, but for technician students it is probably better to identify synthesis as a separate category.

*Synthesis* questions require the student to organise his material and produce an original work. This might be an essay, as in Example 1.4, a computer program, as in Example 1.16, or a design, as in Example 1.17. The form of

## EXAMPLES

### 1.14 *Clothing Cutters/Trimmers*

Give TWO reasons for the use of notches/nips in pattern parts.

### 1.15 *Food Technicians*

A sample of strawberry jam is found by a public analyst to have 60.2% soluble solids. Why would the manufacturer be liable to prosecution?

answer expected may be written, drawing, sketching, calculation or a combination of more than one form and the type of question may be either structured (as in Example 1.17) or unstructured (as in Example 1.16).

*Invention* is a category used by the Technician Education Council, which classifies abilities as information (= recall), comprehension, application and invention. Invention lies somewhere between application and synthesis and may be tested by either structured or unstructured questions. Both Examples 1.16 and 1.17 would be classed as invention under this scheme.

---

## EXAMPLES

### 1.16 *Computer Programming*

A file contains details of magnetic tape files held within a computer installation. Each record consists of the following information

file number
file name
user number
user name
date file first written
file retention period (days)
physical characteristics of tape.

Write a program to read the file and print out, in a suitable format, details of those files whose retention period has passed. You should define how the current date is referred to by the program. At the same time the program should create a new file with those records which have not been printed out.

### 1.17 *Mechanical Engineering Technicians*

An engineering company decides to design and manufacture a 'Wall Light' suitable for general purposes in offices, shops and domestic households. The general design requirements are as follows:

(i) The product is to be easily attached to a wall, with its own off-on switch and be suitably attractive in appearance.

(ii) The unit is to be self-contained and marketed as such.

(iii) Large quantity production is forecast and costs must be kept to a minimum but not to the detriment of the product's appearance and performance.

(a) From the basic information provided and the general requirements of such a product, draw up a list of design requirements giving logical arguments to support each of the items included. (30 marks)

(b) Show any diagrams or calculations required and indicate all assumptions made to justify your design decisions. (15 marks)

(c) Prepare a design layout for the 'Wall Light' giving sketches and written details to show clearly your scheme. (25 marks)

(d) Draw up a parts list for the major components showing from which materials the items have to be made, indicating their finish and/or treatment. Materials of standardised components may be ignored. (15 marks)

(e) Show clearly the design of a package box for transportation of the product to the retailer and consumers. (15 marks)

## APPLICATION

1. Review the types of question used in the written papers of a scheme with which you are concerned. Classify them according to:
   (a) type of question (short-answer, structured, unstructured);
   (b) form of answer (written, drawing, sketching, calculation, graph);
   (c) ability tested (recall, comprehension, application, synthesis).
2. What types of question are not used in your scheme? Could any of these be used with advantage?

# 2

# Why are Constructed-answer Questions Used?

It is undeniable that good objective questions are more reliable than any constructed-answer questions because variations in marking standards are eliminated. In practice objective questions are often more carefully prepared and vetted as well. So, why bother to use constructed-answer questions at all? Why not use objective questions, which are more reliable, or alternatively course-work assessment, which gives better syllabus coverage and avoids examination nerves?

The advantages of constructed-answer questions and the circumstances in which they can best be used may be discussed under the headings of: *validity*; *reliability*; *efficiency*; *side effects*.

## Validity

This concerns the *appropriateness* of the assessment, the extent to which it measures what it is supposed to measure, or what it ought to measure. There are some situations where validity requires the use of constructed-answer questions because they are a more appropriate method of assessment than the alternatives.

Constructed-answer questions are more appropriate than *objective* questions in the following circumstances:

---

**EXAMPLE**

**2.1** *Knitting Machine Mechanics*

A sample of knitted fabric is analysed and found to have a stitch density of 20 stitches per $cm^2$ and a loop length of 7 mm. How much yarn (in kg) with a resultant count of 70tex would be needed to knit a 50 m length of the fabric 1.5 m wide? (Show each stage of your calculation.)

(*a*) if it is necessary to assess the student's ability to produce sketches, scale drawings or graphs;

(*b*) if the student is to be required to follow through a lengthy calculation, as in Example 2.1 (objective questions can of course test short calculations and understanding of the method);

(*c*) if the aims of the course make it necessary to test the student's ability to express himself in writing or to select his material and organise it into the form of an essay;

(*d*) if problems are set for which there is no single correct answer (as in Examples 2.2 and 2.3) or to which there are several possible approaches (as in Example 2.4);

(*e*) if it is desirable that the student should recall the answer for himself and not simply recognise it from the options given; this may be the case with

## EXAMPLES

### 2.2 *Design for Printing*

Two clients both establishing new businesses require letter headings A5 size (210 mm deep × 148 mm wide) which are to be printed by small-offset using two workings. Produce a composing room layout for each heading and explain briefly the reasons for the approach to each design.

COPY
Letterheading A: Knickers and Frocks. Fashion clothes for the under twenties. 147 Queens Lane, London SW1 1NN. Telephone (01) 836 5617.

Letterheading B: Collet, Shaw and Collet. Chartered Accountants. 731 Bowkers Chambers, Evesham, Worcestershire. Telephone Evesham 316. J.L. Collet, FCA, ACCA, P. Shaw, ACCA, T. Collet ACCA.

### 2.3 *Fashion*

Describe and illustrate what could be worn with a cream linen-look blazer to give TWO completely different looks.

### 2.4 *Electronic Components*

The figure below shows the power supply circuit to unit X from a busbar. The supply does not reach X although the busbar is live and the fuse is serviceable. State the most efficient sequence in which to test at the numbered connectors to locate the fault position.

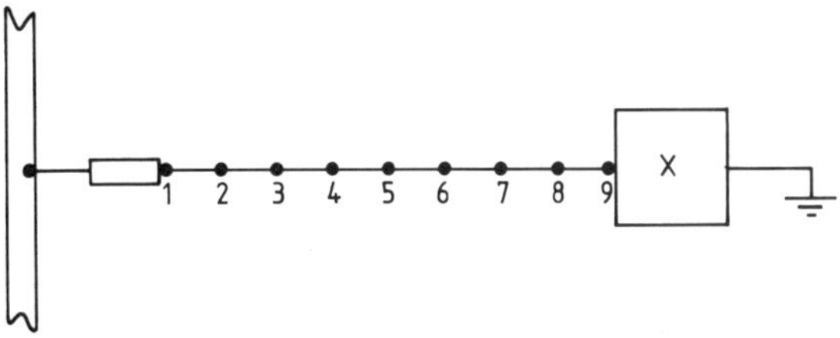

safety and hygiene (see Examples 2.5 and 2.6). Often, however, the *most* important aspect of assessment in such instances is to observe whether the student does in practice follow the correct procedures;

(*f*) if synthesis is to be assessed (as in Example 2.7). It may also prove to be easier and more valid to assess application by constructed-answer questions, although objective questions are often suitable for application.

Contructed-answer questions are usually more appropriate than *course-work assessment* (including projects and assignments) if it is desirable to assess:

(*a*) a student's recall and comprehension of facts without recourse to reference material (for this purpose the assessment might consist of in-course written tests rather than end-of-course examinations);

(*b*) ability to inter-relate knowledge from different areas of the syllabus;

(*c*) ability to retain what has been learnt right up to the end of the course.

## Reliability

This concerns the *consistency* of the assessment method, the extent to which a group of students will get the same results irrespective of when they take the assessment or who examines them.

---

### EXAMPLES

**2.5** *Chemical Technicians*

List FOUR precautions to be observed when cutting glass rod and tubing.

**2.6** *Motor Vehicle Craft*

State the main danger to be avoided when removing road wheels from vehicles employing the divided wheel type of road wheel.

**2.7** *Advanced Cookery for the Catering Industry*

Compile a balanced menu for 100 covers offering the following courses:

(a) a velouté;

(b) a fish course using a whole turbot;

(c) an entreé using rosette of lamb;

(d) roast pheasant with an appropriate salad;

(e) a savoury.

State the correct menu terminology, give a brief dish description and prepare a fully comprehensive stores requisition.

A well-prepared objective test is more reliable than a constructed-answer paper, but where small numbers of students and single colleges are involved, objective tests may lose some of their advantages:

(*a*) good objective questions are difficult to set and if resources are small, poor questions may creep into the test, impairing its accuracy as a measuring instrument;

(*b*) if statistical analysis of the results cannot be attempted for lack of time, or is meaningless because of the small numbers involved, then ensuring comparability of standards from year to year is no easier than with constructed-answer questions.

An examination or test consisting of constructed-answer questions is normally more reliable than a course-work assessment. This is particularly true where more than one college is involved, since it is difficult to ensure that the standards in each are the same, but it is also likely to be true for a single college over a period of years; it is easier to compare a series of examination papers than the course-work of several groups of students when checking on comparability of standards.

## Efficiency

This concerns the 'cost-effectiveness' of the assessment in terms of money, resources, time and effort; an efficient assessment is one which avoids unnecessary work and expenditure of time by lecturer, assessor and student. Objective questions can be marked much more quickly than constructed-answer questions, but require more care and work in the setting. Care is, of course, necessary in setting constructed-answer questions, but unlike objective questions they do not also require the production of four or more carefully worded alternative answers; the outline answers in the marking scheme do not need to be worded with such care. Also, allowances for the imprecision of the question *can* be made in the marking of constructed-answer questions. A constructed-answer paper may be set by a single examiner, but setting the whole of an objective paper is generally considered too great a burden for one person.

Using course-work for assessment usually necessitates extra record-keeping and banking of the exercises set, so that it may require just as much time as setting an examination. Long exercises, such as projects, demand much more student time than examinations, although part of this time is devoted to learning rather than to assessment.

Short-answer and structured questions are more efficient than course-work assessments and projects in that they can achieve good syllabus coverage in a shorter assessment time.

## Side Effects

These are the influences (beneficial or harmful) which the choice of assessment method has upon the course. Over the years the choice of an objective paper as the sole means of assessment is likely to lead to a reduction in the amount of time devoted to the student's ability to communicate in writing or drawing. If these are not an aim of the course, this may not matter. If, on the other hand, ability to communicate is a desirable characteristic in the occupation for which the students are being prepared, then a reduction in the emphasis on it would be an undesirable side effect. This would then be an argument against the use of objective questions.

The use of the 'open book' approach, in which students are permitted to take certain works of reference into the examination, improves the validity of the examination in appropriate cases, and also has important beneficial side effects. If it is known in advance that the works of reference will be permitted, then the teaching of the course can concentrate less on the memorisation of facts and more upon the use and application of the information.

Using an end-of-course examination rather than a course-work assessment may have desirable side effects in stimulating students to work and in ensuring that they retain what they have learnt until the end of the course.

Using an examination method with good syllabus coverage (objective or short-answer or well-prepared structured questions) discourages question-spotting by students or teachers.

APPLICATION

1. Consider the aims of a constructed-answer paper with which you are concerned. List the reasons for using a constructed-answer paper rather than another form of assessment, under the headings of: *validity*; *reliability*; *efficiency*; *side effects*.
2. Does the paper fulfil its aims?
3. Are there any other assessments with which you are concerned which might be more appropriately set as constructed-answer papers?

# 3

# How can Constructed-answer Examinations be made more Valid and Reliable?

Chapter 2 outlined some of the circumstances in which it is more appropriate to use constructed-answer questions than objective questions. Once the decision to use constructed-answer questions has been made, it is necessary to consider what measures can be taken to improve the validity and reliability of the examination, so as to reduce the gap which usually exists between constructed-answer and objective examinations. Some of the techniques which are a well-established part of the process of producing an objective test can equally well be applied to constructed-answer papers, and there are other measures which are peculiar to the latter.

Since the validity of an examination can only really be judged by subject experts, it is important that several such experts, including some who are also familiar with educational measurement techniques, should be involved both in the planning of the examination (see Chapters 4 and 5) and in the 'moderation' of each of the question papers set (see Chapter 10). They should be concerned to see that the examination papers are *valid,* i.e. relevant to the student's course and occupation, in accordance with the specification and appropriate to the student's educational background and to the level of the examination. They should also be concerned to produce an examination which is as consistent and *reliable* as possible. The use of statistical techniques can help in this (see Chapters 15—17 and Appendices).

The rest of this chapter discusses some of the ways in which the quality of a constructed-answer examination can be improved. Of the measures discussed, Nos. 1—11 have a significant effect on the validity of the examination and Nos. 3, 4 and 10—16 affect its reliability.

## 1. Breadth of Syllabus Coverage

If the examination paper is to give an appropriate assessment of the course content it should include questions on as many as possible of the main areas of the syllabus. The use of short-answer and/or structured questions improves syllabus coverage, and these are therefore to be preferred, unless the abilities being assessed require the use of essay or unstructured questions.

## 2. Consistency of Syllabus Coverage

The breadth and balance of the syllabus coverage should be consistent from year to year. This can be achieved by the use of a 'specification' which determines the weightings to be given in the paper to the various syllabus topics and abilities; the same specification remains in force for a number of years, preferably for the life of the syllabus. The drafting of specifications is discussed, with examples, in Chapter 5.

A specification can only be applied if there is a fairly broad coverage of the syllabus in any one examination, so that no major area of the syllabus is omitted; this again points to the use of short-answer or structured questions.

## 3. Elimination of Choice, where Possible

Wherever possible, questions should all be compulsory, as is normal in objective examinations, so that students all take the same 'examination' and are assessed on the same syllabus topics. Offering a choice of questions means that different students may take different 'sub-examinations' based on different syllabus sections and very possibly of unequal difficulty. A choice of six questions out of ten, for example, gives 210 possible different combinations of questions and a choice of 15 out of 20 offers no less than 15,504 possible combinations. Although the offer of a choice of questions sounds attractive, it is not necessarily to the advantage of students, for there is evidence that students do not always choose the questions which they are best qualified to answer. There are, however, circumstances in which an entirely compulsory paper would be inappropriate:

(*a*) If the questions are long and unstructured, it may seem inappropriate to limit students to two or three compulsory questions covering only a small part of the syllabus; such questions might happen to be upon syllabus sections which individual students had missed out or covered inadequately.

(*b*) If the syllabus itself contains options, then the examination based on it cannot be all compulsory. In this case it may be best to divide the paper into sections, with a compulsory Section A and the choice of answering either all the questions in Section B or all the questions in Section C. It may also be desirable to indicate on the certificate or other award which section has been taken, so as to avoid the implication that Section B students are competent in Section C work.

## 4. Equivalence of Optional Questions

It does not matter if compulsory questions are of unequal difficulty—indeed it may sometimes be an advantage. If, however, it is necessary to allow a choice of questions, it is important to try to ensure that the questions are of equal difficulty and marked with equal severity. This is necessary for the reliability of the examination, as well as to ensure that it appears fair to the students. Statistical analysis can help in this, as it is otherwise difficult to judge whether questions will be of equal ease or difficulty. Since any difference in the level of marks awarded to different questions *could* be due, at least in part, to differences in the ability of the students attempting them, it is desirable to have some independent measure of that ability, either in marks for a compulsory first section to the paper, or in marks for a common paper taken by all the students concerned. If the groups of students under consideration are found to have equal average marks on the common section or paper, then it is safe to assume that any differences in the marks awarded to them on the optional questions or section are due largely to differences in the standard of questions or marking, not to the students themselves. It is important, however, to ensure that the common section or paper is equally relevant to both groups of students. If there is no common ground on which both groups can be judged, then it is arguable that they should not be taking the same examination or receiving the same award at the end.

## 5. Appropriateness of Abilities Tested

The specification which determines the syllabus coverage of the examination paper or test (see 2 above) may also be used to help ensure that the abilities assessed are appropriate. Depending upon the nature of the topics assessed, the specification may determine the number of questions or marks which are to be allocated for the abilities of factual recall, comprehension, appplication and (if used) synthesis. Alternatively it may give the number of questions or marks which are to be allocated to written answers, drawings and sketches, graphs and calculations. Forms of specifications and their drafting are discussed in Chapter 5.

## 6. Avoiding Assessment of Irrelevant Skills

In many technical examinations and tests it is important to assess the student's ability to draw, sketch, produce graphs or calculate, and in many business examinations it is important to assess his ability to express himself in English. In other examinations in these fields, however, the main concern is to assess the student's knowledge and understanding of the subject matter of the course and such skills as drawing and writing are involved only as the *medium* of communication and not as an end in themselves.

In such cases it is important to ensure that the examination is indeed assessing the student's technical knowledge and not being influenced unduly by his level of skill in the medium of communication. This point needs to be borne in mind in setting the questions as well as in the marking. It is common to instruct examiners not to deduct marks for poor English or spelling, but if the examination requires long written answers, a student may be penalised by his difficulty in expressing himself in the time available. In other tests, the student who is poor at drawing or manipulating numbers may be similarly penalised.

If the aim of the examination or test is to assess technical understanding, the questions should be designed to elicit evidence of that understanding and to require a minimum of irrelevant skills. Thus a structured question requiring only short answers to each part (as Example 3.1) would be preferable to an essay question such as Example 3.2. A question which provides a diagram and asks questions to test understanding of the circuit or construction shown (as Example 3.3) may be preferable to asking the student to reproduce the complicated diagram from memory.

---

### EXAMPLES

**3.1** *Telecommunication Technicians, Radio and Line Transmission*

(a) Give an application of EACH of the following THREE aerials, stating a typical frequency of operation in EACH case
   (i) half-way dipole with reflector and director
   (ii) unipole
   (iii) ferrite rod.

(b) Describe in detail, with the aid of sketches giving the construction, approximate dimensions and radiation patterns, TWO of the above types of aerial.

**3.2** *Telecommunication Technicians, Radio and Line Transmission*

Discuss the types of aerial in common use.

These comments do not, of course, apply if the aim of the examination is precisely to assess ability to draw, sketch, write or calculate, but care should be taken where there is a dual aim, particularly if writing ability is involved. It is generally better to have two separate assessments, one of technical understanding and one of writing ability, than to try to assess both in one paper. For instance, Example 3.4 is more suitable for assessing essay-writing abilities than for establishing the student's knowledge of specific facts about consumerism and marketing. If both aims are for some reason attempted together, the two aspects should be marked and reported separately, so that the reason for any failure is apparent, and so that good performance in one aspect does not allow a pass to a student who is unsatisfactory in the other.

Even if the main aim is to assess the student's ability to write clear, correct English, it may be appropriate to provide him with a framework for his answer, as in Example 3.5.

## EXAMPLES

**3.3** *Radio, Television and Electronic Technicians*

With reference to the low frequency amplifier stage, shown in the figure below, describe fully the function of:

(a) R1/R2 combination
(b) C1 and C3
(c) R3
(d) R4/C2 combination
(e) R5/C4 combination

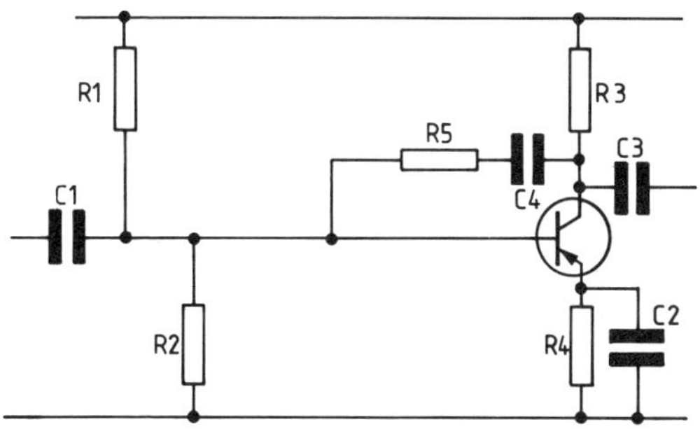


**3.4** *Marketing Management*

'Consumerism is a dynamic environmental factor which raises some vital questions about the nature and scope of marketing in an industrialised society.' Discuss.

## 7. Avoiding Undue Emphasis on Factual Recall

Objective questions are sometimes criticised for excessive emphasis on the recall of trivial factual information, but the same criticism could equally well be levelled at some constructed-answer questions. In both types of examination, the use of an appropriate specification should ensure the inclusion of an appropriate proportion of questions testing understanding and application. In both, but particularly in constructed-answer questions, measures should be taken to provide the student with any information which he will need in order to answer the question, but which he cannot be expected to memorise. One way of doing this is simply to give the relevant data or formulae as part of the question, as in Examples 3.6 and 3.7. This approach has the disadvantage that the student automatically knows which data he needs to use, whereas a more searching and realistic task would be to select as well as apply the appropriate data or formulae. Sometimes, therefore, a list of

---

### EXAMPLES

**3.5** *People and Communication*

(Student is supplied with an extract from a letter of complaint from Mrs Smart, and other relevant information.)

Write a properly laid out letter to Mrs Smart. Make use of the following details and present them in logical order:

(i) Size sent was asked for in order.
(ii) Order received after 'special offer' closing date.
(iii) Refer to colour substitution.
(iv) Subtracted one pair of socks to cover £1.
(v) Says 'M' size in letter but size 'L' in order.

**3.6** *Chemical Technicians*

The wave number of a spectral line is defined as the reciprocal of the wavelength.

(a) Calculate the wave number (in $m^{-1}$) for a line on the hydrogen spectrum whose wavelength is 6562 Å.
(b) What would be the frequency of this line in hertz?

(1Å = $10^{-10}$ m. Speed of light ($c$) = $3 \times 10^8$ m $s^{-1}$)

**3.7** *Heating and Ventilating Technicians*

A room 5 m × 4 m × 3 m high with internal walls and floor has an exposed roof. The roof contains one rooflight 2 m × 1.5 m. Calculate the heat lost to the outside using the following data.

| | |
|---|---|
| *U* for roof | 1.4 W/$m^2$ °C |
| *U* for rooflight | 6.0 W/$m^2$ °C |
| Inside temperature | 20°C |
| Outside temperature | − 1°C |
| Ventilation allowance | 0.15 W/$m^3$ °C |

formulae and constants which *may* be needed is given at the head of the examination paper, the disadvantage of this being that the list may be overlooked or forgotten by the time the student reaches the relevant question. If there is a large amount of information of this type it is often helpful to produce a data sheet giving *all* the information which may be required. It is important to produce such a data sheet at the beginning of the course and to use it in the teaching, so that the students become familiar with its contents and so that the teaching can concentrate on the use of the information contained in it.

## 8. Use of 'Open-book' Examinations

The next stage on from the data sheet is to allow students to take books into the examination. The truly 'open-book' examination in which any works of reference are permitted, is attractive in theory, because it can make the examination more practical and realistic and allow more testing of application. However, it is usually impractical. To allow any books to be taken in would penalise the less wealthy students or make impossible demands on the college's library facilities. It would also necessitate extra space in the examination room to give each student space to stack his books and it might well increase the opportunities for cheating and note-passing. It is usually better to limit the books to one or two with which the student will be familiar in his work and which he can be expected to possess anyway as part of the 'tools of the trade'; works which fall into this category are the *IEE Regulations for the Electrical Equipment of Buildings* for electrical installation students and timetables for travel agency students. The *IEE Regulations,* in particular, contain much information which the student cannot be expected to memorise, but of whose existence he must be aware and which he must be able to apply in practical situations. If the use of the regulations were not permitted in the examination, there would be no means of testing the student's awareness of and application of them.

## 9. Avoiding Undue Emphasis on Speed

In most instances the purpose of the examination is to assess knowledge rather than speed of working, so unless there are special circumstances the examination should be designed so that the majority of students can finish in the time available. If this is to be achieved without loss of syllabus coverage or an excessive increase in examination time, it follows that the questions must be efficient, making the best possible use of the student's examination time. Short-answer and structured questions are more efficient than essay questions.

It is, of course, a waste of examination time to ask the student to do the same thing twice over, for example to perform what is essentially the same calculation with two different sets of figures, as in Example 3.8.

Examination time can sometimes be saved by the use of a combined 'question-and-answer' book, in which the students are required to add to or complete given drawings or graphs. About half an hour would be needed to answer Example 3.9 which is a conventional drawing question requiring the student to set out the drawing for himself. Essentially the same principles could be tested in about 10 minutes by Example 3.10 where the student has only to complete the given drawing. 'Question-and-answer' books can be very useful in extending the coverage of the examination where drawings or graphical work are involved, but are of limited value for written questions and are relatively expensive to produce and bulky to handle.

## EXAMPLES

### 3.8 *Business Calculations*

(a) A 33 lb box of sultanas costs £14.50. What is the price per pound?

(b) Find the cost of one pound of long grain brown rice if 110 lb costs £19.30.

### 3.9 *Sheet Metal Work*

Develop a HALF pattern for the oblique conic frustum shown below. Scale 1:10

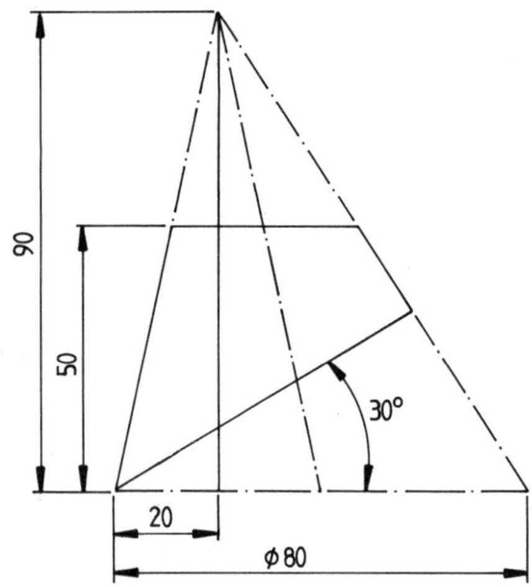

## EXAMPLE

### 3.10 *Sheet Metal and Thin Plate Craft*

Complete the HALF pattern for the oblique conic frustum shown in the figure below.

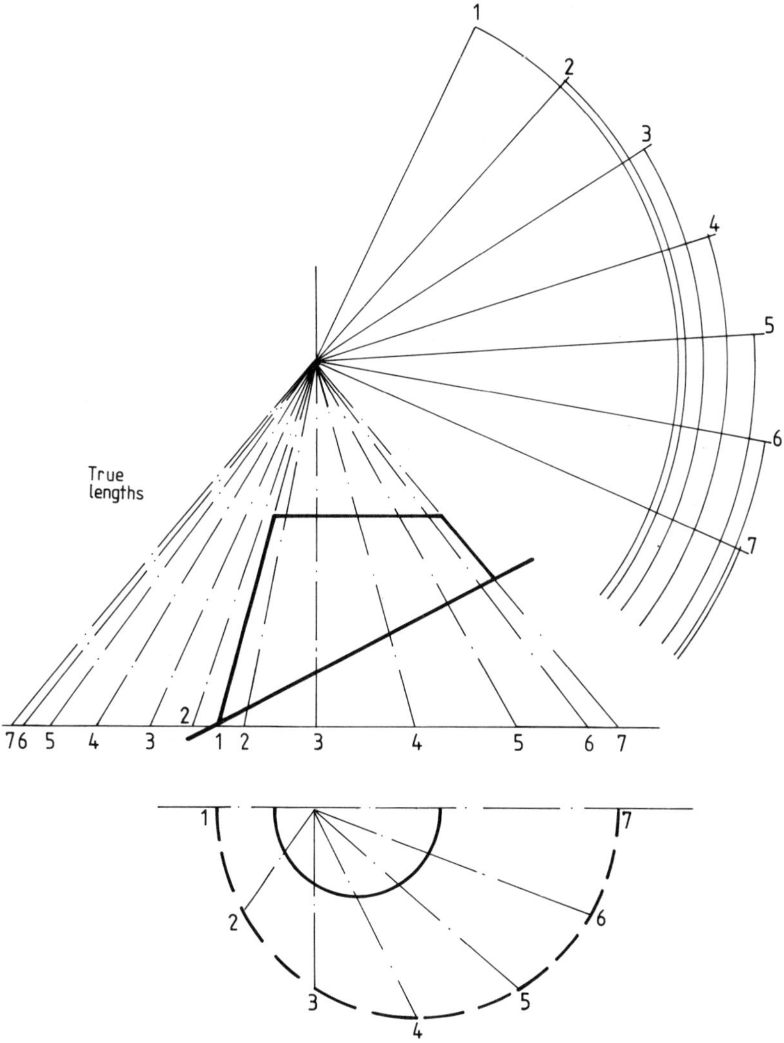

## 10. Clarity of Instructions

The wording of the questions and of the instructions telling students what they have to do must be as clear and explicit as possible, so that all students interpret the questions in the same way. If the question can justifiably be interpreted in two different ways, then the students are in effect answering different questions and being assessed on different bases. Example 3.11 tells the student clearly what he has to do; Example 3.12 leaves him in some doubt as to the nature and scope of the answer required.

## 11. Structuring of Questions

Structuring the questions helps to make clear to the students exactly what is required of them and ensures that all answers follow more or less the same pattern; this in turn facilitates reliability of marking. Consider Example 3.13. The student is given no indication of how many alloys he is to include in his answer or what aspects of them he is to discuss; is he to give exact compositions, methods of production, forms of supply, properties (with numerical values?), advantages, disadvantages, applications, precautions in use? No doubt subject experts would agree on some points which *must* be included, but there are likely to be other points on which their opinions would differ. In any case, the student is left to guess what is expected and may omit information which he knows, simply because he does not realise that it is part of the expected answer to the question. If he includes everything relevant, he may well find himself running short of time later in the

---

### EXAMPLES

**3.11** *Flour Milling*

(a) List THREE major wheat-exporting countries.

(b) For each give
  (i) one wheat type or grade
  (ii) one port of shipment
  (iii) the time of harvest.

**3.12** *Food Technicians*

Write an essay on the significance of the genus salmonella to the food microbiologist.

**3.13** *Sheet Metal Work*

Write a short account of titanium alloys

examination. Consideration of the outline answers to such unstructured questions often shows that an answer including all the relevant points cannot be produced in the time available.

Fresh problems arise when the marker comes to mark the question. If the student has discussed two alloys, the marker does not know whether this was because he did not know of a third or because he considered it less important. If he decides to award full marks to a student who discusses three alloys correctly, what is he to do about a student who discusses four? Is a student who gives a partly incorrect answer under all the headings expected by the marker, to be considered equivalent to one who answers correctly but omits one heading altogether?

Structured questions such as Examples 3.14 and 3.15 avoid some of these problems by giving the students a much better indication of what is required

## EXAMPLE

### 3.14 *Motor Vehicle Craft*

The figure below shows a pump coupling.

(a) State to what part of the injection pump item (1) is connected.

(b) The adjustment bolts item (4) become loose. State the effect this will have on the point of fuel injection (spill point).

(c) A new multi-cylinder, enclosed camshaft, inline fuel injection pump and coupling, are to be fitted to an engine.

State

(i) the method of measuring 'running clearance' of the centre disc,

(ii) how the pump is spill timed and coupled to the engine.

(d) Make a sketch of the service tool which would be used to remove item (1) from the injection pump.

(e) List FOUR effects that retarded pump timing would have on engine performance.

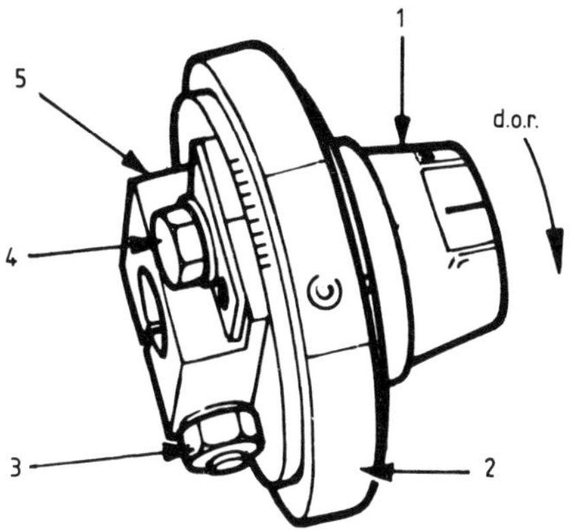

and making the marking more objective. They do not tell the student what the answers are, but indicate what he must do (*state*, *sketch*, *list four effects*, *explain*, *describe*) in order to answer satisfactorily. They also help to ensure that he uses his examination time providing information which the examiner wants.

## 12. Improving Reliability of Marking

Inconsistency in marking is probably the main problem for examiners and lecturers trying to make their examinations and tests match up to the standards of validity and reliability set by objective questions. An objective question is, by definition, one for which there is only one correct answer, so that subjective judgment in the marking is eliminated. By contrast the answer given to a constructed-answer question may be awarded quite different marks by different examiners. This might appear to be unimportant where the numbers of students are small and only one marker is involved, but if the marking is spread over a period of a few weeks, and sometimes even if it is not, the single marker may be inconsistent with himself. If the same question is reused in future years, which assists in the maintenance of the same standard from year to year, then the marking standard may differ from that originally employed, either because a different marker is used or because the original marker has had time to forget the decisions he made the first time.

The problem is not simply a matter of one marker being uniformly $X$% more severe than another; if this were the case it would be easy to make amends by adding $X$ to the mark of each student marked by the severe marker. It is possible for two markers marking the same set of scripts (or an exactly equivalent set) to have the same means (i.e. average marks) but different standard deviations (standard deviation indicates spread of marks — see Chapter 15); the marker with the higher standard deviation will be more

---

### EXAMPLE

**3.15** *Horticulture*

(a) What is meant by the term 'pollination'?

(b) Explain the difference between cross-pollination and self-pollination.

(c) Describe the ways in which flowers may be specially adapted for pollination by
 (i) insects
 (ii) wind.

(d) Give ONE example of a flower which is pollinated by insects and ONE which is pollinated by wind.

generous to the better students but 'mark down' the weaker students. Even worse, the markers may vary in their severity from question to question, so that one marker may be more lenient overall than another, but more severe on one or two of the individual questions; or he may have a higher standard deviation overall but a lower one on some individual questions.

It is obvious then, that as much as possible should be done to improve the consistency and objectivity of marking so as to minimise the variations which may occur. One significant step which may be taken is to improve the structuring of the question as discussed previously (see 11 above). If the question itself is well structured the answers given will all fall into more or less the same pattern, and both ease and consistency of marking are greatly increased. Other measures are given under headings 13 and 14 below.

## 13. Objectivity of Marking Scheme

Consistency of marking requires the use of a marking scheme and this should be prepared in outline at the same time as the question itself, so that the examiner or lecturer is clear at the outset what answers he is expecting and what marks are to be awarded for each part of the answer. If the examiner himself is not clear what answer he is expecting he can hardly be surprised if the students do not know either. The marking scheme will require revision and amplification later, when marking is actually in progress, so as to take account of any unforeseen acceptable answers and to ensure consistent treatment of partially correct ones.

The marking scheme should leave as little scope as possible for the exercise of subjective judgment by the marker, and one important contribution to this is to make the evaluation of each point in the answer an all-or-nothing affair, to be awarded 1 mark or 0, or — if it is considered to be of greater importance — full marks (e.g. 3) or 0. If the marking scheme allows for a point to be marked 'out of 4', then it will be on the answers meriting 1, 2 or 3 that the greatest variation between markers will occur; usually the markers will agree in recognising an answer worth full marks (in this case 4) or a worthless answer, to be accorded 0, but they are likely to differ as to whether a partially correct answer merits 1, 2 or 3. Designing the marking scheme to minimise the opportunities for variation of this sort, depends, of course, on the clarity and precision with which the questions themselves are constructed; a good marking scheme cannot compensate for a poor question.

Example 3.16 shows a clear question and marking scheme. Drafting the marking scheme is considered in Chapter 8 and operating the marking scheme in Chapter 12.

## 14. Coordination between Markers

If there are two or more markers on any one occasion, then measures need to be taken to coordinate their marking, so that any answer will receive the same award whichever of them marks it. The procedures for this are described in Chapter 13.

## 15. Use of Statistical Analysis

Statistical analysis can be used to indicate the degree of difficulty and spread of marks of the examination paper as a whole and to suggest possible instances of variation between markers where this applies (see Chapter 15). 'Dual marking exercises' in which the same batch of scripts is marked by two or more markers (without knowledge of the marks awarded by the other) can confirm any differences and also show which questions have been mainly responsible. Statistical analysis of individual questions (see Chapter 16) can identify questions which are too easy, too difficult or which do not discriminate between the better and the poorer students and this information can be used both for a question banking system and as guidance when writing new questions.

## 16. Question Banking

Banking questions with their marking schemes saves some time in setting questions, but — much more important — it also provides the best available means of ensuring consistency of standards from year to year. If the results obtained in an examination in one year are higher than those in previous years, there is normally no sure means of knowing how far this is because the students are of higher calibre or how far it is because the questions were easier or the marking more lenient. If, however, some of the questions have been used in a previous year, the performance on them in the two years can be

---

**EXAMPLE**

**3.16** *Electrical and Electronic Craft Studies*

*Question*
State TWO functions of the choke in the operation of a switch-start fluorescent lamp circuit.

| *Solution and Marking Scheme* | Marks |
|---|---|
| Produces high voltage pulse necessary to strike or ionise lamp. | 2 |
| Limits the current when the lamp resistance falls. | 2 |

compared and provide a measure of the abilities of the two groups of students. There are three necessary conditions to be fulfilled:

(*a*) Security of questions must be maintained, so that what was a novel problem to the first group of students does not become a matter of rote learning.

(*b*) The questions must not have changed in difficulty or relevance as a result of changes in technology or industrial practice; for example, performance on a question on thermionic valves could not be used as a basis for comparing students now with a group who answered the question in the 1950s.

(*c*) The marking must be as reliable as possible, so as to exclude the possibility of any differences in the level of marks awarded being due to marker variation.

## APPLICATION

Review one or more of the constructed-answer papers with which you are concerned.

1. Does the paper on any one occasion cover a good proportion of the syllabus? Could the syllabus coverage be improved by using a higher proportion of short-answer or structured questions?

2. Is the syllabus coverage consistent from year to year? Is there a specification?

3. Are all the questions compulsory? If not, why not?

4. If there are optional questions for any reason, are they of equivalent nature and difficulty? Is there any statistical evidence to confirm that they are of equal difficulty?

5. What abilities are assessed by the paper? Are they appropriate to the course? Are any relevant abilities not assessed?

6. Does the paper require any irrelevant abilities? In particular, does it demand any *unnecessary* skills in communication — English, drawing, calculation? Could shorter questions or a different format be used to reduce the level of communication skill required?

7. Does the paper overemphasise factual recall? Should any data be provided on the paper or in a separate data sheet?

8. Are any works of reference allowed in the examination? If not, would the

use of some such works make the examination more realistic and more valid?

9. Do the students have difficulty in finishing in time? Are any questions unnecessarily repetitive? Do any involve excessively time-consuming work? Would the use of a combined 'question-and-answer' book help?

10. Are all the questions clear and well structured?

11. Is there a marking scheme? Does it give the minimum opportunity for subjective judgment in marking?

12. Are measures taken to coordinate the marking where necessary?

13. Has any attempt been made to check the consistency of marking by having a set of scripts remarked by a second marker or by the same marker after a time lapse? Were the marks awarded comparable?

14. Has any statistical analysis been undertaken on the paper as a whole or on individual questions? Could such analysis be undertaken?

15. Could question banking be used to improve the reliability of the examination?

PART II

# Planning the Examination

The two chapters in this part are concerned with planning the constructed-answer examination. Chapter 4 concerns the 'examination conditions' which determine such matters as the time allowed, the number of questions to be answered and the availability of reference material. Chapter 5 describes the drafting of the specification which determines the way in which the syllabus is to be covered.

Planning the examination in this way should be undertaken well in advance of the writing of the questions, and ideally when the syllabus content is decided. After all, if successful completion of a course is intended to lead to an award, it is as well to decide at the outset how that 'success' is to be assessed—and indeed to ensure that it can be assessed at all. Once established, the features of the examination should not be changed unless absolutely necessary; this is partly to assist in the reliability of the examination and partly also because students like to know well in advance how they are to be assessed and are disconcerted if they are confronted with an examination paper of an unexpected type. Lecturers who are not themselves the examiners are also likely to be upset if the form or conditions of the examination are changed. If it is found to be really necessary to change the specification or examination conditions, then the change should be publicised well in advance of the examination.

# 4

# Determining the Examination Conditions

The 'examination conditions' relate to such matters as time allowed, number of questions to be answered and availability of reference material. Before any work on setting the paper can begin, decisions have to be made on the following points.

## Type of Question to be Used

Assuming that it has been decided to use constructed-answer rather than objective questions, the decision must now be made whether to use short-answer, structured or unstructured questions, or perhaps a combination. Short-answer or structured questions will normally be preferred to unstructured because of their better syllabus coverage, potential elimination of question choice, greater precision in what is being asked, and greatly superior reliability. They are also the most suitable types of question for assessing factual recall and comprehension. Unstructured questions should be reserved for those situations where the validity of the assessment depends upon the student's establishing the structure of the answer for himself; this may involve organising his material to write an essay, planning and executing a drawing or design, working through a complex calculation, producing a computer program, etc. Even for some of these tasks it may be possible to give a small degree of guidance, so as to set the student working along the right lines, encourage comparability of approach between answers and reduce slightly the burden of marking; Example 3.5 in Chapter 3 showed how students required to draft a letter might be guided to the main points to be included.

The choice between short-answer and structured questions will depend mainly upon the nature of the subject matter and abilities being assessed. If the syllabus is very diverse, then at least part of the paper may need to comprise short-answer questions in order to cover an adequate proportion of the syllabus. Short-answer questions may also be essential if a high proportion of the objectives to be assessed are in the factual recall category. Otherwise the preference will generally be for structured questions because:

(*a*) They can be made more practical and relevant, each question being based on a diagam or a description of a job or a situation. It would not, for example, be an economical use of an expensive-to-reproduce diagram or of the student's examination time to base a single short-answer question on the diagram given in Example 4.1.

---

## EXAMPLE

### 4.1 *Structural and Thick Plate Craft*

The figure below shows two elevations of a column splice connection between two universal columns. The column splice is one of a set of ten, each 8 m in total length.

(a) List a sequence of assembly for completing the splice in the horizontal position.

(b) H.S.F.G. bolts are employed in the completed structure; explain the purpose of the washers which must be used.

(c) State the reason why drilling the web of the column, for location of building and service details, is forbidden.

(d) Describe ONE suitable method of cleaning and protecting the completed column after fabrication.

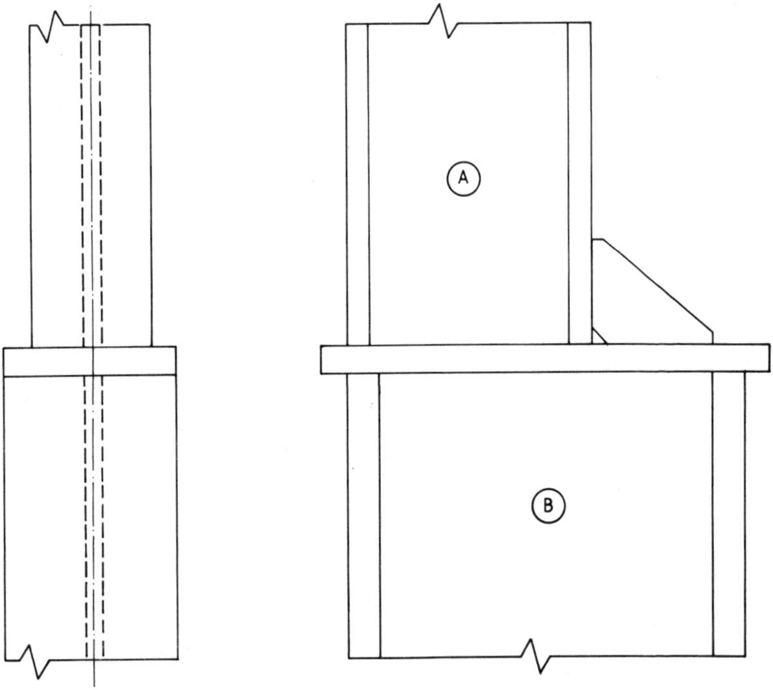

(*b*) It is often easier to assess application of knowledge by structured questions.

(*c*) The student can concentrate on the different aspects of one problem rather than having to switch his mind from one topic to another, as is likely to be necessary in a series of unrelated short-answer questions.

(*d*) Structured questions set around a given problem enable the knowledge acquired under different syllabus sections to be brought together. In Example 4.1 the student is required to use knowledge from several different syllabus areas: sequence of assembly, methods of joining, safety considerations, and surface protection.

Those familiar with the 'item groups' sometimes used in objective tests will recognise that they have many features in common with structured questions; an important difference is that the parts of a structured question may be made dependent upon what has gone before, so making the question more searching.

It is, of course, possible to combine a section of short-answer questions with one of structured questions, so as to get the best of both worlds, if the topics and abilities to be assessed demand this.

## Time Allowed

Other things being equal, the reliability of an examination can be improved by increasing the number of questions (or the number of part-questions if the questions are structured), which implies an increase in the time allowed. Other things are not always equal, however; there is a limit to the length of time for which students can concentrate effectively, and there may in practice be a limit to the number of good, non-overlapping questions which can be set. Hence, the length of the examination cannot be increased indefinitely. It is usual to limit the length of an examination of unstructured questions to 3 hours, although subjects involving longer tasks such as technical graphics may require more time. For short-answer and structured questions, where the spread of syllabus coverage is greater, 2 or 2½ hours will normally be sufficient, and for some syllabuses 1½ hours might be enough. Account must be taken of the amount of syllabus matter to be sampled and the concentrating power of the students involved.

## Number of Questions to be Attempted

It is difficult to give guidance on the number of questions to be required. Up to 10 structured questions may be required in 2½ hours if they involve fairly short answers, but some structured questions require a time allowance of half an hour each. Up to 40 short-answer questions may be required in 2½ hours.

Whatever the time allowance, it is important to be sure that the majority of students can be expected to finish within the time available; if in doubt, set a few comparable questions to a group of similar students and note how long they take.

## Choice of Questions?

The arguments in favour of compulsory questions have already been considered (Section 3 of Chapter 3), and the normal preference should be to make all questions compulsory unless the syllabus itself contains optional sections. It should certainly be possible to make a paper of short-answer questions all compulsory. Structured questions can also usually be made compulsory, at least in a single-college examination, where it can be assumed that the subject matter of all the questions set has been taught during the course. If one section of the usual syllabus has been omitted from the teaching in a particular year, there is little point in including it as one of a set of optional questions, since no one should be attempting it anyway. If the syllabus includes alternative sections requiring that some question choice be offered, there should also be a compulsory section of the examination paper based on the common syllabus sections.

## Division of Paper into Sections

The inclusion of optional sections in the syllabus is one reason why a question paper may be divided into sections. Another is to enable guidance to be given to the student on how to allocate his time during the examination; this is most likely to occur if a combination of short-answer and structured questions is used, when the student will need to know either the relative mark weighting of the two sections or the time allocation for each (these two factors should, of course, go together).

## Marks to be Awarded

If the paper is to be divided into sections, the relative weighting of the sections needs to be decided in advance. For other papers it is generally desirable to decide the mark allocation in advance, so as to be able to prepare a specification (see Chapter 5) and as a guide to those setting questions.

Optional questions must all, of course, carry the same marks. It is not strictly necessary for compulsory questions to carry equal marks provided that the marks for each question are indicated on the paper. If, however, the questions are to be set by more that one person or if they are to be banked for reuse, it is much more convenient for them all to be of equal mark value.

Although many people find it easiest to think in terms of percentages, it is not necessary for the marks for the paper as a whole to total 100; it is often more convenient to use some other total which can be more readily subdivided. For example, a paper of 30 short-answer questions might allocate 3 marks to each question (total 90) or 4 marks per question (total 120); in a paper of 10 structured questions, each question might carry 12 marks, giving a total of 120. It is more convenient to allocate 12 marks to a structured question than 10, because 12 can be more easily divided according to the number of parts in the question (e.g. 2 × 6, 3 × 4, 3 × 2 × 2).

## Use of a Question-and-answer Book

Serious consideration should be given to the possibility of using a combined 'question-and-answer' book if the students are to be assessed on drawing or graphical work. Requiring them to add to or complete a given drawing, sketch

---

**EXAMPLE**

**4.2** *Radio and Television Mechanics*

A Yagi television receiver aerial is shown below. Label the diagram to indicate:

(a) the reflectors

(b) the directors

(c) the direction to the transmitter for maximum signal reception.

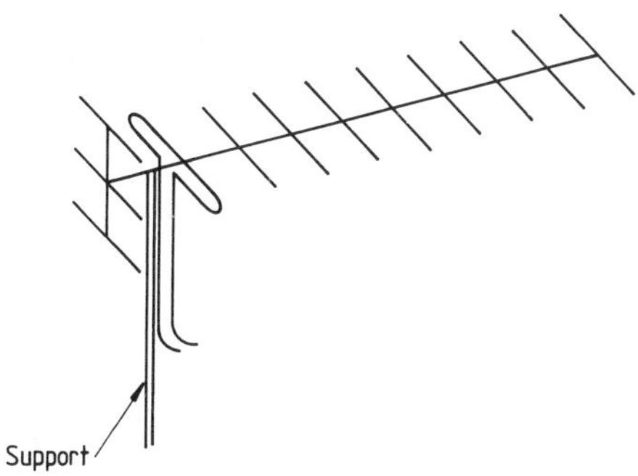

or graph on the examination paper itself (as in Example 4.2) can save much examination time and consequently increase the syllabus coverage of the examination. The advantages are not so great when only written answers are required; even questions originally designed as 'insert questions' where the student is required to fill in the missing word or phrase, can usually be rewritten as straight questions. Example 4.3 is an 'insert question', rewritten as a normal question in Example 4.4

## Requirements for Special Stationery

The nature of the topics and abilities to be assessed will usually determine whether the examination will require the use of such special stationery as

---

### EXAMPLES

**4.3** *Mechanical Engineering*

The figure opposite shows a diagrammatic sketch of a lifting mechanism on a machine tool, where rotation of the handle 'A' causes the platform 'B' to move vertically.
Complete the following statements using one or more words or figures from the table below.

(i) The purpose of the bevel gears is to change the............... of the drive through...............

(ii) One complete revolution of gear 'C' will cause the nut and platform to move one............... of the leadscrew.

(iii) If the handle 'A' is increased in length with a fixed load on the platform 'B', the effort required will be...............

(iv) The force ratio for this system is calculated by

$$\frac{\text{...............moved}}{\text{...............to moved load}}$$

This gives a calculated value of...............

(v) Taking $\pi$ as $\frac{22}{7}$, the effort will move ........ while the load moves 12 mm

(vi) The movement ratio is calculated by

$$\frac{\text{...............moved by...............}}{\text{...............moved by load in the same time}}$$

This gives a calculated value of...............

| | | | |
|---|---|---|---|
| 90°<br>45°<br>60°<br>turn<br>revolution<br>183⅓<br>91⅔<br>366⅓ | pitch<br>lead<br>direction<br>position<br>distance | increased<br>reduced<br>the same<br>effort<br>load<br>efficiency | 4400<br>2200<br>1100<br>10<br>1.0<br>0.5<br>6 mm<br>12 mm |

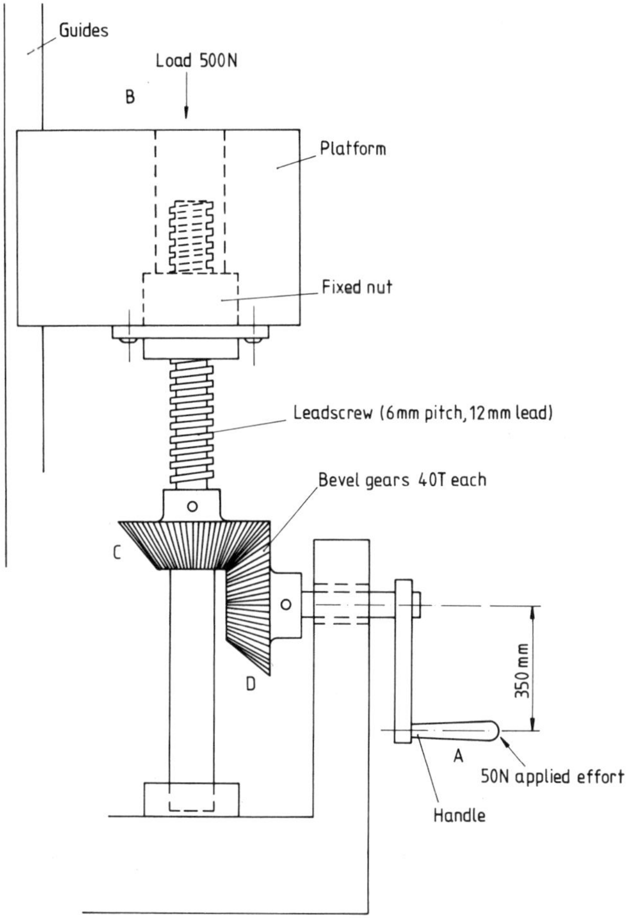


**4.4** *Mechanical Engineering*

(a) Through what angle is the direction of the drive changed by the bevel gears? (OR What is the effect of the bevel gears upon the drive?)

(b) How many leads of the leadscrew will the nut and platform move for one complete revolution of gear 'C'?

(c) What will be the effect on the effort required if the length of handle 'A' is increased, but the load remains the same?

(d) (i) Write down the expression for the force ratio of the system.
(ii) Find the value of the force ratio of the system.

(e) How far will the effort move while the load moves 12 mm? (Take $\pi = \frac{22}{7}$).

(d) (i) Write down the expression for the movement ratio.
(ii) Find the value of the movement ratio.

drawing paper, graph paper or logarithmic graph paper and of associated equipment such as drawing instruments, drawing board and tee square or paints. The use of other special stationery and equipment is illustrated in Example 4.5.

The content of a syllabus indicates where special stationery and equipment are needed and ensures that students become familiar with their use. However, the need for them should be specially noted when the examination is planned, as it may affect the amount of space which each student will require in the examination, and it may be necessary to warn students in advance to bring certain items with them. External examining bodies need also to announce in advance who is to provide the special stationery.

## Use of Aids to Calculation

It has long been common practice in technical examinations to permit the use of slide rules as an alternative to logarithmic tables. The rapid decrease in the price of basic electronic calculators now makes it reasonable to permit their use also. Some reservations must, however, be expressed:

(*a*) For some examinations, particularly at the most basic levels, it may be desirable to banish aids to calculation altogether, so as to be able to assess the student's ability to perform basic mathematical operations competently.

(*b*) Students must be warned, both in advance and on the examination paper, if they must give some indication of the method by which their answer was reached; otherwise it is impossible to give any credit due for correctness of method if the answer is wrong.

---

### EXAMPLE

**4.5** *Retail Bespoke Tailoring*

Draft a block pattern for a lounge jacket 104 breast regular, including sleeve and collar. Do not cut out.

On the pattern produced, mark in contrasting chalks the conversion for a corpulent man with a disproportion of 12 cm at the waist.

Mark ALL measures and style details on the draft.

Student requires:

drafting paper 114 cm × 91 cm
tape measure
black wax or graphite
straight edge, square or curve.

(*c*) Even when calculators are available, there is no merit in setting calculations with complicated figures simply in order to assess understanding of the technology.

(*d*) It may be necessary to impose some restrictions on the use of calculators in examinations, for instance that they must be battery-operated and silent in operation so as not to disturb other candidates.

If trigonometrical or other tables are necessitated by the nature of the syllabus matter it will be necessary to decide in advance of the examination just which edition is to be permitted and who is to provide them.

## Availability of Reference Material

The advantages of permitting the use of data sheets or of other reference material were discussed in Chapter 3, Sections 7 and 8. Since a decision to allow the use of some reference material in the examination will affect the whole teaching of the course, as well as the way in which the questions are set, it is important that such a decision should be made and publicised at the beginning of the course.

Example 4.6 shows a question which makes use of reference material taken into the examination.

APPLICATION

Review the examination conditions for a paper with which you are concerned.

1. Is the type of question the most suitable for the purpose?
2. Does the time allowance accord with the recommendations of the chapter? If not, is there a valid reason for the difference? Can the students concentrate for the length of time required?

---

### EXAMPLE

**4.6** *Structural Engineering Technicians*

A stanchion supports 6 floors and a roof and is spliced 800 mm above the third floor level. The total axial load on the stanchion above the splice is 1000 kN and below 1900 kN. Taking the effective length of the stanchion as 3.6 metres, select suitable uncased stanchion sizes above and below the splice and detail this connection.

Reference material: BS Specifications or BS Codes of Practice and any two design handbooks.

3. Are the number and length of the questions reasonable for the time allowed? Do most students finish the paper in time?

4. Are all questions compulsory? Do optional questions all carry the same marks?

5. Is the allocation of marks to questions and sections fair? Can the marks available for each question be subdivided easily to allow for structuring of the question and marking scheme?

6. Is a 'question-and-answer' book used? If not, would the use of one contribute to validity and efficiency?

7. What special stationery and equipment is required? Does it include everything whose use is required by the syllabus?

8. What aids to calculation are permitted? What other material could, with advantage, be allowed?

# 5

# Devising the Specification

The specification for an examination paper determines the way in which the questions are to be allocated to the different syllabus sections and abilities. Specifications are commonly used for objective papers and it is equally desirable that they should be used, perhaps in a modified form, for constructed-answer questions. Following a well-devised specification ensures that there is an appropriate balance in the coverage of the different syllabus sections and abilities (which contributes to the validity of the examination) and that the coverage is consistent from year to year (which contributes to its reliability).

The specification should ideally be drawn up with the syllabus; the process of drafting the specification may reveal unsuspected deficiencies in the syllabus. Once established, the specification should, if possible, remain unchanged until the syllabus is revised. However, it may be found to need revision after a year or two of operation, particularly if the examiners are not experienced in writing specifications.

The specification may be expressed either in terms of the number of questions to be set on each syllabus topic/ability or in terms of the number of marks for each. The number of questions would be an appropriate basis if the paper consisted entirely of equal-value short-answer questions or of structured questions with each part of equal mark value. The specification determines the allocation of questions or marks to syllabus topics and, according to the requirements of the subject matter, either to forms of answer or to abilities.

## 1. Syllabus Sections

When preparing the specification, it is convenient to divide the syllabus into around 5—10 sections. Fewer than five sections would give too little control over the content of the paper; more than 10—12 sections would give too detailed a specification which would be difficult to operate. The weighting given to each syllabus section should normally reflect both the importance of the topics in it and the time devoted to it during the teaching of the course; however, some basic topics which are essential to the understanding of later parts of the course, may be given a low weighting or even not separately assessed at all. Example 5.1 shows a specification which lays down the number of short-answer questions to be set on each syllabus section, no attempt being made to specify other variables.

Sometimes, if a syllabus is not precisely stated, it may be possible to include some particular topic under more than one section heading. Usually such instances will not become apparent until the questions are written. The paper-compilers will then need to beware of the possibility of including two very similar questions in the same paper under different headings.

## 2. Form of Answer

It may be desirable to specify the number of questions or marks to be allocated to answers in different forms, i.e. *written answers*, *drawings or sketches*, *calculations*, *graphical answers*.

If this division is not specified, there may be a tendency for the paper to include too many calculations which are easy to set and to mark. Alternatively, the paper might concentrate too much on written work, testing knowledge which could be more reliably tested by objective questions and neglecting the skills of drawing and graphs which may be the very reason for the existence of the constructed-answer paper.

Even if the specification is not expressed in terms of the form of answer required, it may be necessary to place a limit on the total number of questions or marks to be allocated to each form.

---

### EXAMPLE

**5.1** *Masonry*

| Heading | | No. of questions |
|---|---|---|
| 1. | Functions, principles of elements | 5 |
| 2. | Materials | 4 |
| 3. | Methods | — |
| 4. | Tools/equipment | 3 |
| 5. | Measurement/setting out | 5 |
| 6. | Safety | 3 |
| 7. | Protection, preservation, insulation | 4 |
| 8. | Testing, inspection, fault-finding | 5 |
| 9 | Communication | 1 |
| | | 30 |

## 3. Abilities

The specification may determine the allocation of questions or marks to the abilities of factual recall, comprehension and application (these were defined in Chapter 1). Sometimes invention and synthesis may also be included, although these abilities are more likely to be tested in a separate paper, for which a different form of specification may be appropriate (see page 50).

Example 5.2 shows a question which tests factual recall—simply whether or not the students can remember the names of the acids described.

Examples 5.3 tests comprehension — whether or not the student understands the reasons why pitting may occur.

Example 5.4 tests application — the student's ability to apply his knowledge and understanding to a problem which is new to him (although it need not necessarily be new to the lecturer also); in this case the problem is the drafting of a pattern under specified conditions.

Since the classification of abilities is in the form of a hierarchy, each ability normally includes those below it in the hierarchy. Thus comprehension usually includes an element of factual recall and application usually requires that the student remembers and understands in order to be able to apply his knowledge. It is often difficult to assign questions to their ability category with complete certainty, but the attempt is worth making in order to ensure, for example, that the paper does not contain an excessively high proportion of factual recall questions.

---

## EXAMPLES

### 5.2 *Bread Making and Flour Confectionery Technicians*

(a) Name the main acid present in each of the following:

- (i) sour milk
- (ii) vinegar
- (iii) lemons.

(b) Name the acid which is formed when ethanol (ethyl alcohol) is oxidised.

### 5.3 *Electrical Epilation*

Give THREE reasons for pitting of the skin due to epilation. State how such damage can be avoided.

### 5.4 *Knitting Machine Mechanics*

Draft a simple two-colour jacquard pattern for a double system power flat machine. The pattern width is limited to 18 needles and the depth controlled by 6 jacquard steels which rotate in the following repeat sequence:
1, 2, 3, 4, 5, 6, 5, 4, 3 and 2.

If the syllabus is written in the form of examination objectives, it is much easier to decide which types of ability the paper should test and the weightings for each.

## A Specification using Number of Questions

Example 5.5 shows the type of specification which might be used for a 40-question short-answer paper. Each 'cell' in the specification represents the number of questions to be set on the indicated topic and ability; for example, only one question is to be set testing recall of facts on the components section of the syllabus, but two testing recall on the machines section and four testing comprehension on the machines section.

It is not necessary to have questions in each possible subdivision; for example, no questions are considered necessary for application of knowledge on either machines or related science.

The right-hand column shows the total number of questions to be set on each topic and the bottom row shows the totals for each ability.

A similar specification could be used for a paper consisting of eight structured questions, each with five equal parts.

## A Specification using Number of Marks

Example 5.6 shows a different form of specification, in which each 'cell' shows the number of marks to be allocated to each topic and form of answer.

### EXAMPLE

**5.5** *Specification for a Paper containing 40 Short-answer Questions*

| Topic | Abilities | | | Total |
|---|---|---|---|---|
| | Factual recall | Comprehension | Application | |
| Components | 1 | 1 | 2 | 4 |
| Machines | 2 | 4 | 0 | 6 |
| Systems | 2 | 4 | 2 | 8 |
| Legislation/ regulations | 4 | 2 | 2 | 8 |
| Testing and fault finding | 2 | 0 | 6 | 8 |
| Related science | 2 | 4 | 0 | 6 |
| Totals | 13 | 15 | 12 | 40 |

This form of specification would be more appropriate for a structured paper in which the part-questions carried unequal marks. In this example the marks for the paper are assumed to be 100, although there is no reason why this need be so; the specification could equally well show total marks of 120 or any other figure. In this case also there is no need for an entry in every cell; in the example given it is assumed that graphical questions will be set only on the related science section of the syllabus. Where a specification is written in terms of the syllabus topic and form of answer, it may be desirable to place some overall limit on the number of questions to be set testing each ability; for example, the specification might carry the rider 'not more than 30 marks to be allocated to questions testing recall'.

The characteristics shown in Examples 5.5 and 5.6 can be interchanged. For example, it would be possible to devise a specification expressed in terms of the number of questions to be set for each topic and form of answer or one which defined the number of marks to be awarded to each topic and ability.

## A Simplified Specification

It may sometimes be found too restricting to work to a specification which lays down the number of questions or marks for each 'cell'. A simpler form of specification such as is given in Example 5.7 may therefore be preferable. This example, which is in fact a simplified version of Example 5.6, gives the total marks to be awarded for each topic and for each form of answer, but does not allocate marks to each cell of the grid. It does, however, indicate by means

**EXAMPLE**

**5.6** *Specification for a Paper Marked out of 100*

| | Form of answer | | | | |
|---|---|---|---|---|---|
| Topic | Written | Drawing/ sketching | Calculations | Graphical | Total |
| Materials | 10 | 0 | 0 | 0 | 10 |
| Tools and equipment | 5 | 5 | 0 | 0 | 10 |
| Working methods | 15 | 5 | 0 | 0 | 20 |
| Measurement and setting out | 0 | 15 | 5 | 0 | 20 |
| Work planning | 15 | 0 | 5 | 0 | 20 |
| Related science | 5 | 0 | 5 | 10 | 20 |
| Totals | 50 | 25 | 15 | 10 | 100 |

of an asterisk, those cells on which it is appropriate to ask questions, showing, for example, that only written answers will be required to questions on the materials section. A specification of this type is easier to operate, but still ensures an appropriate balance between the different topics and between the different forms of answer.

Simplified specifications could also be used for topics and abilities and could be expressed in terms of number of questions rather than number of marks.

## Specifications for Papers Testing Invention or Synthesis

The types of specification described above may not be appropriate for papers testing synthesis or invention; because the questions are usually longer, good

### EXAMPLES

**5.7** *Simplified Specification for a Paper Marked out of 100*

| | Form of answer | | | | |
|---|---|---|---|---|---|
| Topic | Written | Drawing/ sketching | Calculations | Graphical | Total |
| Materials | * | | | | 10 |
| Tools and equipment | * | * | | | 10 |
| Working methods | * | * | | | 20 |
| Measurement and setting out | | * | * | | 20 |
| Work planning | * | | * | | 20 |
| Related science | * | | * | * | 20 |
| Totals | 50 | 25 | 15 | 10 | 100 |

**5.8** *Specification for Paper Testing Invention or Synthesis*

| | Marks |
|---|---|
| Correct identification of the elements of the problem | 20 |
| Appropriateness of solution | |
| feasibility of solution | 20 |
| attractiveness of design | 10 |
| use of appropriate materials | 10 |
| use of appropriate production methods | 10 |
| economy of materials and labour | 10 |
| compliance with regulations or Codes of Practice | 10 |
| compliance with other safety considerations | 10 |
| Clarity and accuracy of drawings | 20 |
| Accuracy of calculations | 20 |
| Total | 140 |

syllabus coverage may be impossible in any one examination paper, and the emphasis is on the student's use of information in problem-solving, rather than on his recall or comprehension of facts. For such a paper it may be preferable simply to list the abilities which the student is expected to show in answering the problems set, as in Example 5.8. The marks to be allocated to each ability in each paper may be given either as single figures, as shown, or as a range (e.g. 10—20).

## APPLICATION

1. Review the specification for a constructed-answer paper with which you are concerned.
   (a) Does it ensure an appropriate balance between different syllabus topics, forms of answer and abilities? Should it be more specific?
   (b) Is it easy to work to in practice? If not, how could it be modified?
2. Draft a specification for a paper which does not already have one. Ask a colleague to comment on its suitability, including the practicality of working to it.

PART III

# Producing the Examination

The chapters in this part deal with the process of actually writing and producing the examination paper — all the stages which must be completed before the students sit the paper. It is assumed, however, that the planning stages described in Part II have already been completed — the examination conditions have been decided and the specification agreed.

Chapter 6 of this part, which is perhaps the most important chapter of the book, describes the points which must be observed when writing the questions in order to make them as valid and reliable as possible. Chapter 7 discusses additional points which must be considered when writing questions for an open-book examination. Chapter 8 discusses the drafting of the marking scheme, something which must be regarded as integral to the production of the examination paper. The marking scheme must be drafted with the question if the writer is to be sure that the question can be answered and can be reliably marked. The drafting of the marking scheme is therefore considered in this part, although its updating and operation are considered in Chapter 12 (Part IV). Chapter 9 lists the points to be observed when putting the questions together into a paper and preparing the instructions to students. Chapter 10 looks at moderating — what it is, why it is necessary and what points should be considered. Finally, Chapter 11 considers the layout of the paper, including 'question-and-answer' books, and the care needed when having it duplicated.

# 6

# Writing the Questions

Writing the questions for an examination requires knowledge of the subject matter, knowledge of the students and their capabilities, knowledge of the standard required, and adherence to some general principles of question writing, which are listed below.

## 1. Choose a Topic which is within the Syllabus and Specification

This seems an obvious point, but it is not unknown for questions which appear in drafts and even in actual examinations to be outside the syllabus. If more than one lecturer or college is involved, there may be differences in interpretation of the syllabus and the questions set must take account of the consensus interpretation. This is one of the reasons why moderation of the question paper is important (see Chapter 10).

It is, of course, much easier to ensure that the questions accord with the general interpretation of the syllabus if the syllabus itself is clearly written, preferably in terms of objectives, and if the specification is well-designed, and available to all the lecturers concerned.

The abilities tested by the question and the form of answer required must also accord with the specification. For example, if the specification does not envisage the use of calculations in questions related to materials, then a question of that nature would be inadmissible.

## 2. Test Knowledge which is Important

It is possible for a question to be within the syllabus and specification and yet still be unsuitable if the knowledge or abilities which it is tests are trivial or irrelevant or if the information is too abstruse to be expected knowledge. Example 6.1 shows a question which seems to be testing rather trivial information for a technician examination, particularly as the question does not ask for reasons for the suitability of the materials chosen.

## 3. Make the Questions Practical and Relevant

As far as possible, the questions should be, and should be seen to be, practical and relevant to the student's occupation or motive for study. Questions on principles should normally be related to a practical application and the figures given in a calculation question should be realistic (see Example 6.2) if this can be done without making the working unnecessarily complex. The provision of diagrams, maps and pictorial information, of the type which the student is likely to meet in his job, makes the questions more valid and more obviously relevant (see Example 6.3). This point is perhaps more important at craft level, but should not be overlooked at technician level.

## 4. Avoid Testing Irrelevant Abilities

Examination questions not infrequently make irrelevant or only partly relevant demands upon the student. The most obvious example is the essay

### EXAMPLES

**6.1** *Refrigeration Technicians*

Give ONE example of the use of EACH of the following materials in a component of a refrigeration system.

(a) Grey cast iron
(b) Low carbon steel
(c) Stainless steel
(d) Soft annealed copper . . . etc.

**6.2** *Carpentry and Joinery*

Calculate the cost of materials for a stair from the table given, adding 5% for waste.

| Item | No. | Length mm | Breadth mm | Thickness mm | Cost per Lin. m |
|---|---|---|---|---|---|
| Treads | 13 | 900 | 240 | 32 | £1.00 |
| Top nosing | 1 | 900 | 75 | 32 | 30 p |
| Risers | 14 | 900 | 180 | 15 | 34 p |
| Strings | 2 | 4200 | 260 | 38 | £1.25 |
| Wood for corner blocks | 1 | 3000 | 63 | 63 | 50 p |
| Wood for wedges | 1 | 1100 | 100 | 10 | 14 p |

question which requires the student to select and organise his facts and express them in prose, even though the examiner may be primarily interested in his knowledge of particular facts. If a calculation question is designed to assess the student's understanding of the relationships between quantities, then there is no need to use complicated figures which test also his arithmetic ability. In Example 6.4 the figures given are unnecessarily complex and the

## EXAMPLE

**6.3** *Motor Vehicle Craft Studies, Electricians*

The figure shows a windscreen wiper motor.

(a) What type of field system is used in this motor?

(b) State ONE advantage of using this type of motor.

(c) How is the rotation of the armature converted into the reciprocating motion necessary to operate the wiper arms and blades?

(d) How is two-speed operation achieved in this type of motor?

(e) State TWO functions of the component labelled 3.

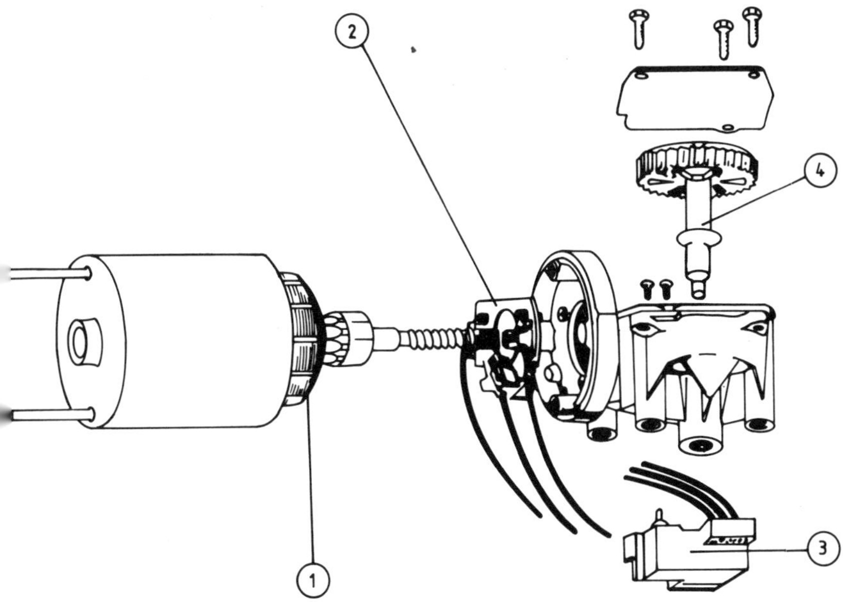

essential understanding could be better assessed if the figures were 2 H, 2 V, 5 A, 12 A. Better still would be to choose some figure other than 2 for either *L* or *V*, as it would then be much easier to see during marking what method the student had used.

If the student's understanding of the workings of a circuit is more important than his ability to draw the circuit from memory, then a question such as Example 6.5 is to be preferred to 'Draw the circuit of a valve oscillator and explain how it works'. Example 6.5, which asks specific short questions is also

---

## EXAMPLES

### 6.4 *Electrical and Electronic Craft*

In a coil of 2.3 H inductance an applied voltage of 1.7 V raises the current from 4.9 A to 11.8 A. Find

(a) the rate of change of current

(b) the time required.

**SOLUTION**

$V = L \times$ rate of change of current

$$\text{Rate of change of current} = \frac{V}{L} = \frac{1.7}{2.3} = 0.74\ \text{A/s}$$

$$\text{Time required} = \frac{11.8 - 4.9}{0.74} = \frac{6.9}{0.74} = 9.32\text{s}$$

### 6.5 *Electrical and Electronic Craft*

The figure below shows a valve oscillator.

(a) How is the oscillation initiated?

(b) How is the necessary positive feedback obtained?

(c) What is the purpose of the components *Cg* and *Rg*?

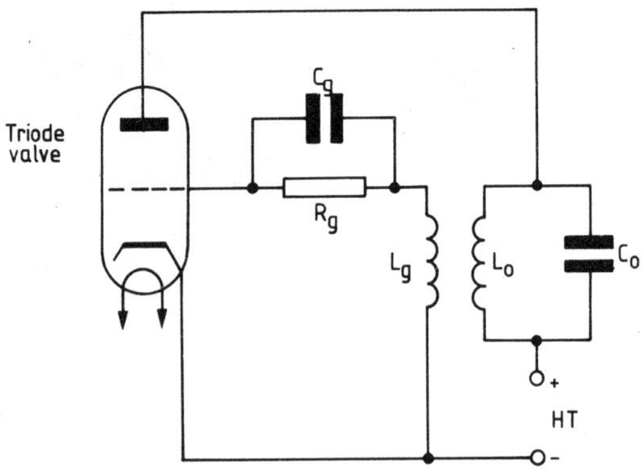

to be preferred, in most cases, to 'Explain the workings of the circuit shown in the diagram.

It is also necessary to guard against the danger of making questions so complex that they test the student's ingenuity and intelligence rather than his knowledge of the subject matter.

## 5. Don't give the Student Unnecessary Work

Since examination time is limited, it is sensible to make the best possible use of it, and not to involve the student in unnecessary work. One way of using the student's examination time efficiently is to provide a graph or diagram for completion as in Examples 6.6 and 6.7. This may be just as valid an assessment as requiring him to draw everything himself, and may well also allow more reliable marking.

## 6. Avoid Unnecessary Repetition

It is usually a waste of the examinee's time to require him to answer several part-questions, each of which tests essentially the same knowledge and abilities. Example 6.8 requires the student to carry out no less than eight simple calculations, each of which is the same except for the figures involved; the additional two sections at the end differ only slightly from the first eight.

This sort of repetition is most likely to occur with calculations, but can also

---

### EXAMPLE

**6.6** *Electrical Craft Studies*

The figure shows a cathode ray tube. Label the components marked (a), (b) and (c), and state the function of each.

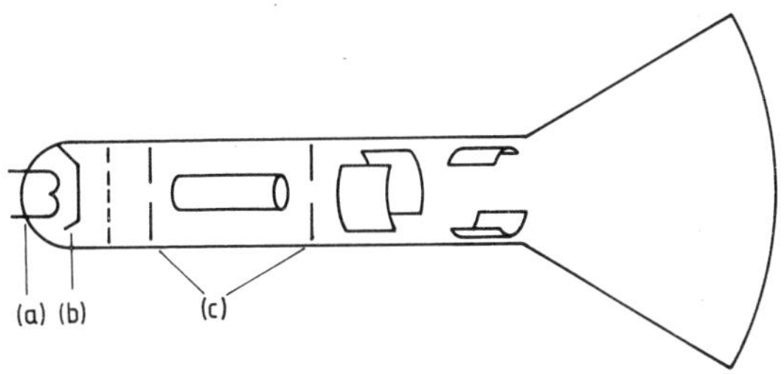

## EXAMPLE

### 6.7 *Mechanical Craft Studies*

The table lists the spindle speeds in rev/min of a Pillar Drilling machine

| TABLE | | | | | | | | | |
|---|---|---|---|---|---|---|---|---|---|
| Speed number | 1 | 2 | 3 | 4 | 5 | 6 | 7 | 8 | 9 |
| Spindle speeds | 70 | 90 | 140 | 205 | 280 | 395 | 540 | 750 | 1060 |

Plot the speed number/spindle speed graph below

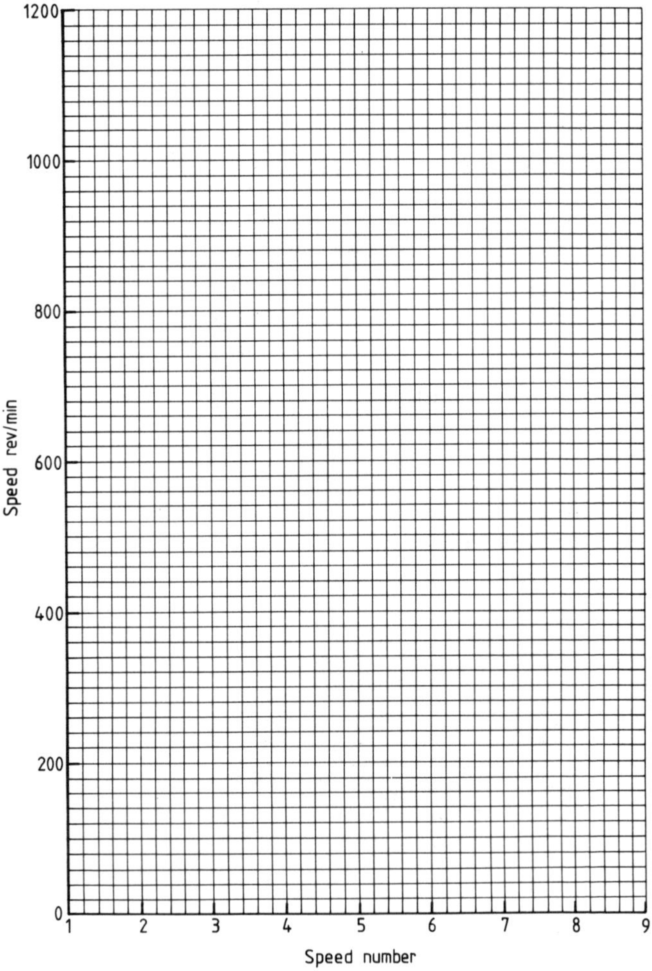

## EXAMPLE

**6.8** *Mechanical Craft Studies*

The increase in length (expansion) of a material depends on three factors

(1) Original length of the component $L$ (mm)
(2) Coefficient of linear expansion $\alpha$ (constant)
(3) Temperature change $\delta\theta$ (°C)

The factors are connected by the following formula

expansion $x = L \times \alpha \times \delta\theta$ (mm)

Using this information complete the following tables by

(a) listing the following materials in order of their ability to expand the largest amount by calculating the expansion and inserting numbers 1—4 in the last column (1 indicating the greatest expansion).

| MATERIAL | ORIGINAL LENGTH $L$ | TEMPERATURE RISE $\delta\theta$ | COEFFICIENT OF LINEAR EXPANSION $\alpha$ | EXPANSION $x$ mm | ORDER |
|---|---|---|---|---|---|
| Aluminium | 100 mm | 100°C | $24 \times 10^{-6}$/°C | | |
| Copper | 100 mm | 100°C | $17 \times 10^{-6}$/°C | | |
| Mild Steel | 100 mm | 100°C | $12 \times 10^{-6}$/°C | | |
| Brass (60/40) | 100 mm | 100°C | $20 \times 10^{-6}$/°C | | |

(b) calculating the expansion of the following components and inserting the values in the last column.

| COMPONENT | ORIGINAL LENGTH $L$ | TEMPERATURE RISE $\delta\theta$ | COEFFICIENT OF LINEAR EXPANSION $\alpha$ | EXPANSION $x$ mm |
|---|---|---|---|---|
| A | 1000 mm | 100°C | $24 \times 10^{-6}$/°C | |
| B | 1500 mm | 50°C | $17 \times 10^{-6}$/°C | |
| C | 1200 mm | 300°C | $12 \times 10^{-6}$/°C | |
| D | 1500 mm | 100°C | $20 \times 10^{-6}$/°C | |

(c) inserting the correct values in the blank spaces of the table below showing details of components X and Z involved in an expansion process.

| COMPONENT | DIMENSION | TEMPERATURE | | COEFFICIENT OF LINEAR EXPANSION $\alpha$ | EXPANSION $x$ mm |
|---|---|---|---|---|---|
| | | INITIAL TEMP. | FINAL TEMP. | | |
| X | 1000 mm length | 15°C | 95°C | $12 \times 10^{-6}$/°C | |
| Z | 50 mm diameter | 15°C | | $20 \times 10^{-6}$/°C | 0.065 |

occur in written and drawing questions. Examples 6.9 and 6.10 also appear excessively repetitive and Example 6.10 has the further disadvantage that it involves the student in drawing four circles when the purpose of the question is presumably to assess technical understanding.

## 7. Make the Question as Clear and Concise as Possible

The wording of the question should be as clear and concise as possible. Often, as in Examples 6.11 and 6.12, the use of a diagram is shorter and clearer than a verbal description would be. As a general rule, particularly for lower level courses, irrelevant information and comment should be excluded. Sometimes, however, at higher levels, part of the point of the question may be to assess the student's ability to select relevant information from that provided. If the information is given on the examination paper rather than in material allowed into the examination, the student should be warned, either on the paper or in advance, that he may not need to use all the facts supplied.

### EXAMPLES

**6.9** *Refrigeration Technicians*

Write down the correct abbreviation to BS 308 for EACH of the following terms:

(a) across flats
(b) countersunk
(c) counter bore
(d) diameter
(e) hexagon
(f) internal diameter
(g) material
(h) not to scale
(i) outside diameter
(j) pitch circle diameter.

**6.10** *Photographic Technicians*

Draw diagrams to represent the appearance of a circle coloured as shown below, when viewed through EACH of the following filters:

(a) cyan
(b) blue
(c) red
(d) magenta.

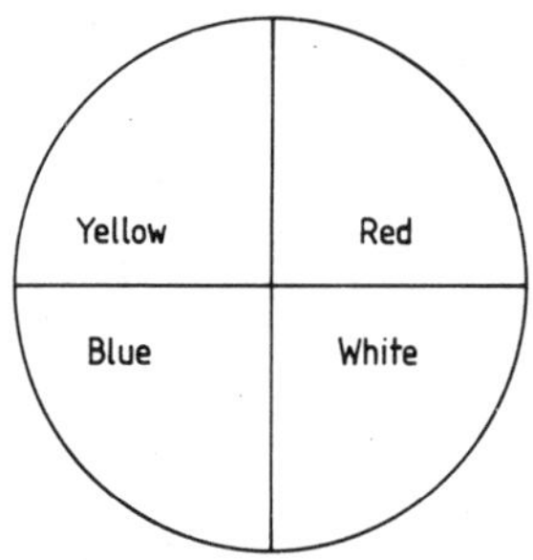

## 8. Arrange the Question in a Logical Order

This applies particularly to calculation questions. Example 6.13 shows how *not* to arrange such a calculation; the student needs to find the cost of ingredients for one person (c) before answering (a) and (b).

### EXAMPLES

**6.11** *Electrical Craft Studies*

Calculate the resonant frequency for the circuit shown below.

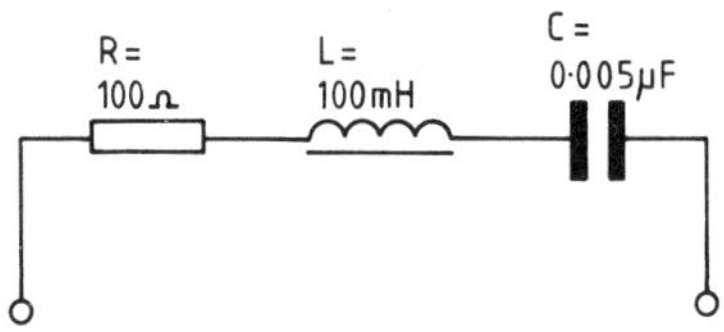


**6.12** *Heating, Ventilating and Air Conditioning Technicians*

The figure below shows a lever TWO metres long. A load of 4.8 kN is to be balanced by an effort of 1 kN. Determine the distance of the fulcrum from the load.

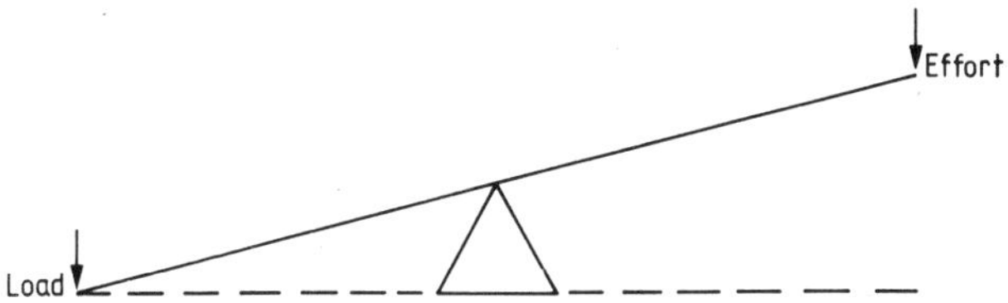


**6.13** *Catering*

(a) The cost of ingredients for a meal for 6 people is £4.20. What would be the cost for 11 people?

(b) A similar meal in a restaurant costs £3.50 per person. What percentage of the total cost of the restaurant meal are the ingredients?

(c) What is the cost of ingredients for one person?

In Example 6.14 the parts of the question are arranged in the order in which the student needs to tackle them.

Example 6.15 shows a non-calculation question in which the parts are arranged in a logical order.

## EXAMPLES

### 6.14 *Mechanical Technicians*

The figure below shows the segment of a circle ABCDA. Calculate:

(a) the distance OD
(b) the area of the triangle ACO
(c) the angle $\theta$
(d) the area of the sector OABCO
(e) the area of the segment ABCDA.

(No marks will be awarded for a solution obtained by measuring a scale drawing.)

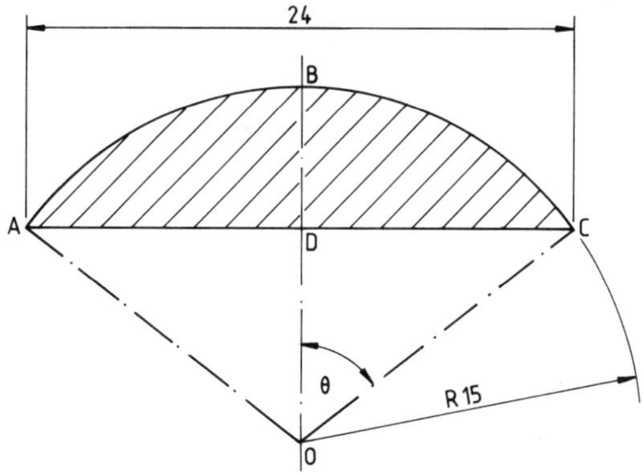


### 6.15 *Painting and Decorating*

A decorative device is to be acid etched into a sheet of glass, and the glass is to be subsequently gilded. State:

(a) what type of acid is used for the etching
(b) in what type of container the acid is stored
(c) how the etched glass is prepared for gilding
(d) what form of gold leaf is used for glass gilding
(e) ONE type of mordant used for glass gilding
(f) what the mordant is mixed with to prepare it for use
(g) the name of the thin brush used to convey the leaf to the surface
(h) what is meant by 'faulting' the gold
(i) how the gold is fixed where required before the surplus gold is washed off
(j) what is used to protect the edges of the gilding from subsequent damage.

## 9. Make Quite Clear what the Student has to do

Unless it is a specific aim of the question to assess the student's ability to structure his own answer, the question should give him as much guidance as possible concerning what he has to do.

(*a*) The scope of the answer should be indicated. Where possible specific questions should be asked (see Example 6.5, page 58). Otherwise the main headings for the answer should be suggested. Examples 6.16 and 6.17 are poor in this respect, because the student may be left in some doubt as to the sort of information which the examiner requires. In Example 6.16 is anything required in the 'notes' other than a description of the method and an example of a mixture for which it is suitable?

Example 6.18 is an improved version of Example 6.17. Examples 6.19 and 6.20 also show how the main headings of the answer may be

---

### EXAMPLES

**6.16** *Science Laboratory Technicians*

Write notes on FOUR of the following methods of chemical separation, giving ONE example in each case of a mixture for which the method is particularly suitable.

(a) diffusion
(b) filtration
(c) fractional crystallisation
(d) chromatography
(e) sublimation
(f) steam distillation.

**6.17** *Footwear Craft Studies*

Write notes on TWO materials commonly used in footwear manufacture.

**6.18** *Footwear Manufacture Technicians*

For EACH of TWO of the following

crepe
p.v.c.
resin rubber
polyurethane cellular unit

describe:

(a) production (b) properties (c) applications

**6.19** *Electrical and Electrical Installation Technicians*

Describe the measurement of resistance using the Wheatstone Bridge principle. Set out your answer in the form of a laboratory report, which should include a circuit diagram, details of the equipment used, procedure, typical results and conclusions.

suggested, giving the student a better indication of what is expected, and making the task of marking easier.

(*b*) The form of the answer should be indicated. Sometimes a complete answer needs to include both written work and diagrams and this should be indicated to the student, as in Examples 6.21 and 6.22. This approach is usually preferable to 'Describe, with sketches where appropriate . . .'.

Mathematical questions should indicate whether solutions may be found graphically — this is implied by the term *find* but excluded by *calculate.*

(*c*) The number of points expected for a complete answer should usually be stated. Example 6.23 is unsatisfactory in this respect, because the student does not know how many factors he is expected to list. Example 6.24 is preferable.

## EXAMPLES

### 6.20 *Horticulture*

Describe the production of a crop of winter lettuce in a heated glasshouse, for marketing in December in a specified area of the country. Use the following headings:

(a) plant raising, including dates
(b) soil preparation and planting
(c) temperature regimes and watering
(d) carbon dioxide enrichment.

### 6.21 *Roadwork*

(a) Sketch an elevation of an arched masonry bridge and indicate the following:
(i) extrados
(ii) intrados
(iii) keystone
(iv) spandril
(v) voussoirs
(vi) abutment

(b) (i) List FOUR defects which could occur in masonry bridges.
(ii) State briefly the remedial treatment for EACH defect.

### 6.22 *Construction Services Welding*

A butt weld is to be made between two lengths of 50 mm diameter low carbon steel pipe in the fixed vertical position by the rightward technique.

(a) Make a sketch showing the joint set-up, direction of travel and angles of filler wire and blowpipe.
(b) State FOUR advantages of using the rightward technique in preference to the leftward technique.
(c) Explain the difference in joint edge preparation and welding procedure if the leftward technique had been specified.

### 6.23 *Carpentry and Joinery*

List the various factors which govern the development or reduction of pressure of concrete within formwork. State which of the factors result in increased pressure and which assist by reducing pressure.

Occasionally, however, particularly in safety questions, the student may be required to know how many points there are to list, for example 'State the safety precautions which should be observed when . . .'.

(*d*) The length of the answer expected should be suggested, either by a statement of the number of marks allocated, or by the wording of the question. *State*, *list* and *name* indicate that short answers only are required — see Examples 6.25 and 6.26. *Describe* and *discuss* suggest that longer answers are expected, as does *explain*; *explain* should, however, be used with care, as it implies that more than a mere description is involved. Example 6.27 should probably read *describe* rather than *explain*, unless the student is actually expected to explain the reasons for the procedure outlined, in which case the question should say so explicitly.

Example 6.28 is unsatisfactory, because *Write a short account of* implies that several points are expected under each heading, but as only 4 marks are allocated to each heading, little more than a description can be expected.

## EXAMPLES

**6.24** *Basic Cerificate in Computer Programming*

Give THREE advantages of magnetic tape compared with magnetic disc as a backing storage device.

**6.25** *Science Laboratory Technicians*

List THREE excretory systems in the mammal, stating in EACH case TWO of the main substances excreted.

**6.26** *Electrical Craft Studies*

State the essential difference between a maintained and a non-maintained emergency lighting system.

**6.27** *Construction Services Welding*

Explain the recommended method of lighting up an oxy-acetylene flame.

**6.28** *National Distribution Certificate*

Write a short account of EACH of the following:

(a) pedestrian shopping precincts

(b) hypermarkets and superstores

(c) cash and carry wholesaling

(d) door-to-door selling

(e) direct mailing shots.

A drawing or sketching question may need to state the features to be included, as an indication of the scope of the answer and the length of time to be spent — see Example 6.21 above.

(*e*) The use of the word 'you' is generally considered to be poor style in examination papers, since a question which asks *How would you do*. . . can be answered correctly by the student who describes his own method, whether or not it is generally considered correct or feasible. A correct and truthful answer to Example 6.29 could well be 'Nothing'. Example 6.30 also invites a very subjective answer and is unlikely to provide much information about the student's knowledge or understanding of the subject.

## 10. Make it Easy to Identify Errors when Marking

This applies particularly to calculation questions. Listing the stages required in the calculation, as in Example 6.14 above, enables the marker to see, if necessary, where the student has gone wrong and to give credit for those stages which are correct. This is especially important if slide rules or electronic calculators are permitted.

Marking is also easier if the figures given differ from one another; this was mentioned in connection with Example 6.4. If $V$ is 2 $V$ and $L$ is 2 $H$ and the student writes down

$$\text{Rate of change of current} = 2/2$$

the marker does not know whether the student intends this to be

$$\frac{V}{L} \text{ or } \frac{L}{V}$$

If, however, $L$ is given as 2 $H$ and $V$ as 4 $V$, the marker can see which way up the student has the expression, even if he does not quote the formula.

### EXAMPLES

**6.29** *Catering*

What do you know of the Hotel and Catering Industry Training Board?

**6.30** *Flower Arrangement*

How do you see your role as a flower arranger in relation to the world-wide movement for conservation of the countryside?

Example 6.31 also shows how marking may be made easier. Requiring the student to state the page of the tables which he is using enables the marker to follow through his calculation and award credit for correct *use* of the table, even if the wrong table has been chosen.

## 11. Avoid Making Later Parts of a Question too Dependent upon Earlier Parts

This is likely to occur in calculation questions, but can usually be compensated in marking. In other types of question, however, such as Example 6.32, failure in the first part of the question may make it impossible

### EXAMPLES

**6.31** *Electrical Installation*

A load of 38 A is supplied from a 240 V, 50 Hz single-phase supply by means of a 2-core p.v.c. armoured cable having copper conductors. The cable is situated in an ambient temperature of 35°C and is clipped to a wall. The length of run is 15 m and close excess-current protection is provided.

Using the IEE tables,

(a) State the
- (i) table to be used
- (ii) correct columns of current rating and voltage drop
- (iii) rating factor for the class of protection
- (iv) rating factor for the ambient temperature.

(b) Calculate the
- (i) maximum permitted voltage drop
- (ii) minimum size of cable which may be used.

**6.32** *Motor Vehicle Craft Studies*

(a) What type of combustion chamber is shown in the figure below?

(b) State the type of injector nozzle used in this chamber.

(c) What is the operating pressure for this injector?

(d) Why is 'air-swirl' necessary?

(e) State TWO methods that can be used to promote 'air-swirl' in this type of chamber.

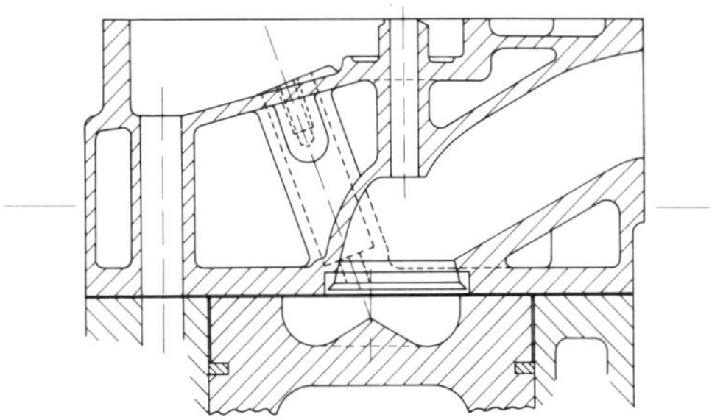

to gain credit for some or all of the later parts. This particular example proved difficult, and the moderators subsequently decided that it would have been better to state the type of combustion chamber in the question, so as to give the students a start.

## 12. Ensure that there is a Solution which can be Provided within the Time Allowed

This is another obvious point which is sometimes overlooked, either in setting the question or in checking the typing. Examples 6.33 and 6.34 show two questions which cannot be answered: 6.33 because the information given is contradictory and 6.34 because it is inadequate. Checking that the question can be answered in the time available involves working through the solution or answer, allowing extra time for the student, who will not have the advantage of knowing beforehand what is in the examiner's mind. A second opinion is useful here (see Chapter 10 on moderating).

### EXAMPLES

**6.33** *Mathematics*

Construct a right-angled triangle with sides 30 mm, 40 mm and 60 mm long.

**6.34** *Horticulture*

A rectangular plot 20 m long is to be planted at 12.5 cm × 12.5 cm.

(a) Calculate the number of plants required.

(b) Calculate the quantity of fertiliser required at 70 $g/m^2$.

**6.35** *Mechanical Technicians*

A sample of 60 items was checked on a particular dimension and allocated to categories as follows.

| Dimension $x$ mm | 49.5 to 49.7 | 49.7 to 49.9 | 49.9 to 50.1 | 50.1 to 50.3 | 50.3 to 50.5 |
|---|---|---|---|---|---|
| Frequency | 4 | 14 | 24 | 14 | 4 |

(a) State the mean value of $x$.

(b) Show that the standard deviation is 0.2 mm.

(c) Presuming that a batch of 1000 similar items has the same mean and standard deviation, estimate the number of items in the batch where the dimension $x$:
   (i) lies between 48.8 and 50.2
   (ii) lies over 50.1
   (iii) lies between 49.6 and 50.0.

Use the following values of the area under the curve of normal distribution:

| Range | $-0.5\sigma$ to $+0.5\sigma$ | $-\sigma$ to $+\sigma$ | $-1.5\sigma$ to $+1.5\sigma$ | $-2\sigma$ to $+2\sigma$ |
|---|---|---|---|---|
| Area | 0.382 | 0.682 | 0.866 | 0.954 |

## 13. Supply any Necessary Data

The examiner should ensure that any data which the student needs in order to answer the question is available to him, either in reference material taken into the examination or in information supplied in the question paper. Example 6.35 provides information on the characteristics of the normal distribution,

### EXAMPLE

**6.36** *Traffic Engineering Technicians*

In the table shown below are the results of a survey of vehicle speeds measured on a suburban road before and after the imposition of a 40 mile/h speed limit.

| Speed range (mile/h) | Number of vehicle speeds observed in the speed range: before limit | after limit |
|---|---|---|
| Less than 14 | 0 | 0 |
| 14–18 | 3 | 5 |
| 18–22 | 4 | 9 |
| 22–26 | 8 | 10 |
| 26–30 | 10 | 13 |
| 30–34 | 18 | 18 |
| 34–38 | 18 | 27 |
| 38–42 | 30 | 36 |
| 42–46 | 31 | 30 |
| 46–50 | 32 | 21 |
| 50–54 | 35 | 20 |
| 54–58 | 21 | 12 |
| 58–62 | 10 | 5 |
| 62–66 | 7 | 2 |
| 66–70 | 2 | 0 |
| More than 70 | 0 | 0 |

Has the imposition of the speed limit significantly reduced vehicle speeds?

Use the following formulae and the Student *t* table [not reprinted here] to help you decide.

$$\bar{x} = \frac{\Sigma fx}{\Sigma f}$$

$$s^2 = \frac{\Sigma fx^2 - \Sigma (fx)^2/n}{n - 1}$$

$$t = \frac{\bar{x}_1 - \bar{x}_2}{\sqrt{\dfrac{s_1^2}{n_1} + \dfrac{s_2^2}{n_2}}}$$

which the student is expected to be able to use but not to memorise. Information in this category may sometimes include complex formulae — see Example 6.36. It is often helpful to identify the data required for a question by grouping it all at the end of the question, with the heading *Data*.

## 14. Use Preferred Units, Abbreviations and Terminology

The units and abbreviations for quantities used will depend upon the requirements of the particular occupation concerned. For most subject areas metric units are now used and a very useful reference work for correct practice is *SI Symbols, Abbreviations and Conventions* published by the Council of Technical Examining Bodies. The terminology used should also accord with current correct practice in the industry or occupation concerned.

Example 6.37 gives a small number of instances of preferred and non-preferred usage.

Drawings and symbols should accord with British Standards or other relevant authorities.

Trade names should be avoided, if possible, as should jargon not likely to be familiar to the student.

## 15. Ensure that Adequate Stationery is Available

The examiner should ensure that appropriate stationery will be available, particularly if there is a need for graph paper or drawing paper. He should

---

### EXAMPLE

**6.37** *Preferred and Non-preferred Terminology*

| Preferred | Non-preferred |
|---|---|
| 6.6kV | 6.6-Kv |
| 240V a.c. | 240-V AC |
| 10 rev/s | 600 r.p.m. |
| 0.2 Ω | .2 Ω |
| cage-rotor induction motor | squirrel-cage motor |
| a.c. generator | alternator |
| capacitor | condenser |
| low carbon steel | mild steel |
| tungsten-arc gas-shielded | T.I.G. |

also check that the size of paper which is specified will accommodate the answer to the question without difficulty — drawings and graphs may go off the edges of the paper if too large a scale is stated in the question.

## APPLICATION

1. In the light of this chapter, review a constructed-answer paper you have set recently (or one with which you are concerned). Does each question conform with all the recommendations of this chapter?

2. Rewrite the paper or individual questions as necessary.

3. Write new questions to test any desirable topics or abilities not covered by the paper.

4. Write new questions for any of the following categories not already included in your paper
   (*a*) a question using a diagram, map or other pictorial information;
   (*b*) a question in which the student is given a graph, diagram or similar to complete;
   (*c*) a structured question (calculation or similar) consisting of a series of steps arranged in logical order;
   (*d*) a question supplying data or formulae for use by the student when answering.

# 7

# Setting Questions for Open-book Examinations

Most of the points listed in Chapter 6 apply to open-book examinations, but in addition there are some special points which need to be considered when planning open-book examinations and when setting the questions.

## 1. Give Adequate Notice of the Rules

Students and lecturers need to know well in advance — preferably at the beginning of the course — what information will be permitted in the

---

### EXAMPLE

**7.1** *Examples of information permitted in examinations*

**Construction and Construction Services**
Building Regulations
Construction (Health & Welfare) Regulations
The Standard Method of Measurement of Building Works
BS Specifications, BS Codes of Practice and design handbooks (for structural engineering)
Flow of fluids in pipes and ducts (extract from *IHVE Guide*)
Mayhew & Rogers: *Thermodynamic and Transport Properties of Fluids*
*IEE Regulations for the Electrical Equipment of Buildings*

**Engineering**
Data sheet BS 4500A *Selected ISO Fits — Hole Basis*

**Travel**
Timetables, brochures, rail map, *ABC World Airways Guide*

**Law Papers**
Legal textbooks and reference books

**Language Papers**
Dictionaries

**General**
Mathematical tables
Ready reckoner

examination. One of the major advantages of the open-book approach is that it allows the teaching of the course to concentrate on the application of facts rather than their memorisation, and this advantage would be lost if students and lecturers did not know until late in the course what information would be allowed in the examination. Students also need the opportunity to familiarise themselves with the information which will be used. Often this consists of tables or regulations with which they are expected to be familiar as part of their job, but sometimes (as with data sheets or specially prepared tables) the information is in a form which they would not otherwise meet, and they need the opportunity to find their way around it.

Colleges will also need to know well in advance whether they are required to provide unmarked copies of the material or whether students may take in their own copies. If the examination is designed to test application of information rather than recall, then students can normally be allowed their own copies, whatever annotations they may have made on them. Some examples of information which may be permitted in examinations are listed as Example 7.1.

## 2. Ensure that the Reference Material is Used

Students who are expecting to be able to use certain reference material in the examination are likely to be disconcerted if they are denied it or if there is no opportunity to make use of it. If the information is sufficiently important to justify the initial decision to allow it in the examination, then it is probably sufficiently important to be used in every examination.

## 3. Recognise the Need for Adequate Time

The timing of the examination and the length of the questions should be such as to give an advantage to the student who is familiar with the reference material, and able to find his way around it easily. However, it must be recognised that under the pressure of an examination students find a strong temptation to spend time checking facts they already know, so as to be absolutely sure. Consequently, a little extra time should be given to allow for this.

## 4. Test Application of the Information

Although the examiner will want to reward familiarity with the reference material, there is usually little point in setting questions which can be answered by just looking up and copying out a portion of the reference material. Example 7.2 is arguably poor in this respect, since the student has only to look in the timetables available to find the answer. Example 7.3 is better because it involves using the information available and applying it to a particular situation.

In Example 7.4 the information needed to answer the question can only be extracted from the regulations in the time available by someone who is already fairly familiar with their layout and contents.

For Example 7.5 the student needs to refer to the tables at the end of the *IEE Regulations for the Electrical Equipment of Buildings*; these give the current

---

## EXAMPLES

### 7.2 *Travel Agency*

Which two French ports are linked to Southampton by car ferry?

Reference material includes ferry timetables.

### 7.3 *Travel Agency*

Mrs S. Pinnock would like to visit her daughter in Boston, USA. She has been reading about fare reductions but is confused by APEX, SUPER APEX, STANDBY, BUDGET, ABC and EXCURSIONS. She comes to your office on 15 August and asks for the cheapest fare for the following journey

| | |
|---|---|
| London—Boston | 28 September |
| Boston—London | 20 October |

She cannot change these dates.

(a) What type of fare is best for Mrs Pinnock?

(b) How much will it cost?

(c) List FIVE differences betwen ABC flights and excursion flights.

(d) How much would she have to pay if she cancelled her bookings on 10 September?

(e) What would she be charged if she travelled one way, London—Boston on 28 September?

Reference material—*ABC World Airways Guide*

### 7.4 *Construction Technicians*

A building project is planned to take two years to complete and employ not more than 50 men on site at any one time.

Briefly describe the following temporary site provisions

(a) direct cold water and 250 litre heated water storage

(b) sanitation

(c) electricity supply for the site lighting and portable power tools

(d) welfare provisions

Reference material—Building Regulations and Construction (Health and Welfare) Regulations

rating and voltage drop for various sizes of copper and aluminium cables, with factors which have to be applied in particular circumstances.

Example 7.6 shows a question designed to be answered with the aid of a specially prepared data sheet, which the students also use during the course. The information contained in the data sheet includes surface area of a cone, volume of cone and conic frustum and trigonometrical ratios.

## 5. Do not Test Obscure Information

The use of works of reference in the examination allows the examiner to test the student's awareness of, and ability to use, a much greater range of information than would be assessed in a conventional examination. However, the temptation to make the examination more difficult by asking for obscure information should be avoided, if it is information which the student is unlikely ever to need to use.

APPLICATION

1. Review an open-book examination with which you are concerned.
   (*a*) What reference material is permitted in the examination? Is it used?

---

**EXAMPLE**

**7.5** *Electrical Installation Technicians*

(a) Compare the use of cables with aluminium and copper conductors with respect to
   (i) cost
   (ii) installation
   (iii) termination.

(b) A p.v.c. armoured four-core cable, 80 m long and clipped directly to a surface is to be used to supply a balanced three-phase load of 29 kW at 0.8 lagging power factor from a 415V supply. The ambient temperature is 25°C, coarse protection is to be used and the voltage drop is limited to 2%. The price of 1000 m of four-core, copper conductor, armoured cable is given in the following table.

| Conductor Cross Section | Price |
|---|---|
| 16 $mm^2$ | £1745 |
| 25 $mm^2$ | £2330 |
| 35 $mm^2$ | £2980 |
| 50 $mm^2$ | £3955 |

If aluminium conductor cables of the same conductor size are 20% cheaper, in order to satisfy the conditions stated above, find
   (i) the smallest copper conductor cable
   (ii) the smallest aluminium conductor cable
   (iii) the cheapest cable of (i) and (ii) above.

(*b*) Do the students have enough time to answer the questions?

(*c*) Do the questions test application of the reference material or merely the ability to find facts from it?

(*d*) Do the questions test any obscure knowledge the student is unlikely ever to use in practice?

2. (*a*) Which of the examination papers with which you are concerned could profitably allow the use of reference material? List the material which might be allowed, including data sheets.

(*b*) What effect would the use of this material have on:
   (i) the validity of the examination;
   (ii) the teaching of the course?

## EXAMPLE

**7.6** *Foundry and Patternshop Technicians*

A ladle, used for casting aluminium alloys, has the dimensions shown below. Calculate

(a) the surface area of the metal in contact with the ladle
(b) the angle $\theta$
(c) the mass of the alloy in the ladle if the relative density is 2.5.

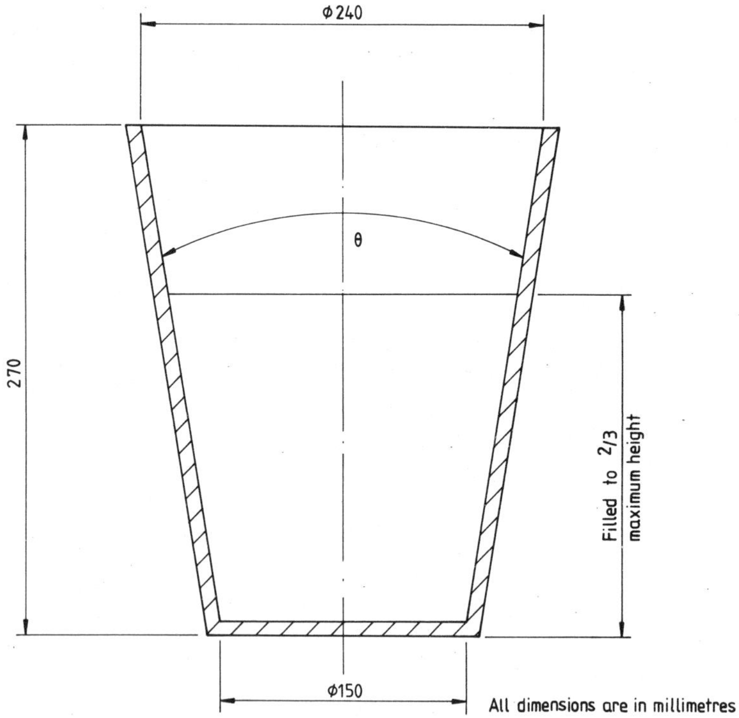

# 8

# Drafting the Marking Scheme

An outline answer and marking scheme should be prepared at the same time as the question and certainly before the questions are submitted to an assessor or a moderating committee. The marking scheme may need amendment as a result of changes made by the moderators, and will certainly need amplification when marking is actually in progress (see Chapter 12). However, there are good reasons why an outline answer and marking scheme should be prepared with the question:

(*a*) It ensures that there *is* an answer, that there is a solution to numerical problems and that (for example) there are two points which can be made where two are asked for.

(*b*) It helps both the examiner and the moderators to assess the time required to answer the question and the level of difficulty.

(*c*) It helps to ensure that there is an appropriate relationship between time taken, work done and marks awarded.

(*d*) Consideration of these points may indicate that some revision of the question itself is desirable.

(*e*) The outline answer and marking scheme help the moderators to appreciate the intent and scope of the question.

(*f*) The answer provided may show that the wording of the question does not convey what the examiner intended to ask — if no answer is provided then there is no check that each moderator is not interpreting the question in a different way.

(*g*) Provision of answers helps both examiner and moderators to assess the extent of syllabus coverage of the paper.

For questions requiring written answers, the full answer need not be written out at this stage, but the outline should include the main points expected, the number of points required to obtain maximum marks (this should, of course, usually be apparent from the question) and the marks for each part — see Example 8.1.

For numerical questions, a full solution should be provided with the question, showing marks for each stage of the calculation and indicating the relationship between marks for method and marks for computational accuracy (see Example 8.2).

## General Points

The following points apply to the provision of outline answers and marking schemes, whatever the form of the answer required.

(*a*) The marks awarded to each question or part-question should bear a relationship to the work done by the student and to the importance and difficulty of the topic. It is unjust for equal marks to be awarded for work of unequal length or difficulty, particularly in a paper offering a choice of questions. Examples 8.3—8.6 all come from the same paper and are optional questions, each carrying 5 marks, but there is an apparent unevenness in the amount of work involved; Example 8.3 seems to need only a fairly brief answer, whereas 8.6 requires three diagrams; Example 8.4 is so vaguely worded that the student has no means of knowing how many answers are expected.

(*b*) It may well prove difficult to set a series of short-answer questions each requiring the same amount of work. However, equality is not necessary if

---

### EXAMPLE

**8.1** *Coal Preparation Practice*

List FIVE of the optimum conditions necessary for the efficient operation of a mechanically sound Baum-type jig.

**Marking Scheme**
Any FIVE of the following

Uniform feed rate and composition
Mobile bed with uniform jigging action
Uniform feed distribution over the full width of the bed
Elevators not overloaded
Correct level of washing water in the tower
Avoidance of too strong or too weak pulsation and suction strokes
Regular checking of bed thickness
Regular inspection of the products
Cut off air supply under 'no feed' conditions
Control the solids content in the washing water
Regular inspection and maintenance of equipment

2 marks each for any 5 10

the questions are compulsory — different mark allocations can be made according to the amount of work involved provided that the mark weighting for each question is shown on the paper. For optional questions, of course, the marks awarded must be the same, and

## EXAMPLES

### 8.2 *Coal Preparation Practice*

(a) Calculate the relative density of a suspension of 5 volumes of water, 2 volumes of coal slimes (RD 1.4) and 1 volume of magnetite (RD 5.0).

(b) Would a piece of coal of mass 210 g with a volume of 150 ml float or sink in this mixture?

| | **Marking Scheme** | | | | Marks |
|---|---|---|---|---|---|
| (a) | Mass of water | $= 5 \times 1$ | $= 5.0$ | | |
| | Mass of coal slimes | $= 2 \times 1.4$ | $= 2.8$ | method | 2 |
| | Mass of magnetite | $= \frac{1}{8} \times 5$ | $= 5.0$ | accuracy | 1 |
| | | | $12.8$ | | 1 |
| | Relative density of suspension | | $= \frac{\text{mass}}{\text{volume}}$ | | 1 |
| | | | $= \frac{12.8}{8}$ | | |
| | | | $= 1.6$ | | 1 |
| (b) | Relative density | $= \frac{\text{mass}}{\text{volume}}$ | | | |
| | | $= \frac{210}{150}$ | | | |
| | | $= 1.4$ | | | 1 |
| | The coal will float | | | | 1 |
| | | | | | 8 |

### 8.3 *Embroidery*

What is 'bebilla' work and where does it come from?

### 8.4 *Embroidery*

Give the names and localities of stately homes in Britain where famous Elizabethan embroideries are to be found. Name some of these embroideries.

### 8.5 *Embroidery*

What are the characteristic features of Elizabethan dress embroidery design? Name TWO techniques and THREE stitches used in this work.

### 8.6 *Embroidery*

Give diagrams to illustrate rice, renaissance and rococo stitches.

consequently the length and difficulty of the questions must also be the same.

(*c*) The number of marks available should be related to the number of points expected in the answer. This is important, both from the point of view of obvious fairness and also for reliability of marking. Example 8.7, which awards one mark for three answers, and Example 8.8, which awards three marks for two answers, are likely to give problems in the marking of partially correct answers. The marker may well be inconsistent with other markers and even with himself in deciding what to award to a student who has got the question half or a third correct. Examples 8.4—8.6 are also unsatisfactory in this respect. In these examples a consideration of the marking scheme should lead the examiner or moderators back to a reconsideration of the question itself.

(*d*) Fractional marks should be avoided, being difficult to handle and likely to lead to errors in addition. Half-marks may occasionally be necessary; other fractions should never be used.

(*e*) Provision must be made for marking anything which is required by the question. Example 8.9 is at first sight satisfactory; five fruits are required and one mark is awarded for each. However, the question asks for a

---

## EXAMPLES

### 8.7 *Beauty Therapy*

State a suitable temperature for the use of EACH of the following:

(a) sauna bath

(b) steam bath

(c) paraffin wax. (1 mark)

### 8.8 *Chemical Technicians*

Give TWO instances in which chlorinated rubber compositions might be recommended as a paint system. (3 marks)

### 8.9 *Catering*

List FIVE fruits which might be used to make a suitably varied fresh fruit salad in July.

**Marking Scheme**

Any 5 of

| | |
|---|---|
| apple | orange |
| apricot | pineapple |
| banana | plum |
| cherry | raspberry |
| dessert gooseberry | strawberry |
| grapes | |

(5 × 1 mark 5)

selection which could be used to make a *suitably varied* fresh fruit salad, so one or two additional marks should be allocated for the suitability of the *combination* of fruits listed.

(*f*) Marks must not, of course, be allocated for anything which is not clearly required by the wording of the question. Example 8.10 asks the student only to name the teeth involved, but the marking scheme expects the number of each sort and the order to be stated. If these are really required, a better wording for the question would be 'Name and chart the teeth . . .'.

(*g*) In technical examinations marks should not normally be awarded for neatness, spelling, correct English or similar factors. There are, however, some technical subjects and more business subjects in which one of the aims is precisely to test the student's ability to communicate in writing; in other subjects neatness of drawing may be required. Great care should, however, be exercised when allocating marks to such qualities, as they are likely to involve a very subjective judgment by the examiner.

(*h*) The marking scheme for any question should allow the minimum possible scope for subjective judgment on the part of the marker. This is obvious if there are two or more markers, but is also important if there is only one marker who may spread his marking over several sessions, or if the questions are to be banked for reuse. The allocation of up to 5 marks for a part-question, as in Example 8.11, invites the marker to award intermediate marks (one, two, three or four) to answers which are only partly correct. Inconsistencies are likely to occur, and it is difficult to judge the relative worth of two different, partly correct answers. In Example 8.11 the question itself is at fault and a much more precise version is needed; this is in fact an instance where an objective question would almost certainly be preferable. In other situations the marks available should be limited to one per point or, if a point is considered to

---

## EXAMPLE

### 8.10 *Dental Technicians*

Name the teeth which make up the set of temporary ('milk') teeth.

**Marking Scheme**

| | |
|---|---|
| 8 incisors | 2 |
| 4 canines | 2 |
| 8 molars | 2 |
| Correct order | 2 |
| | 8 |

be worth two marks, the marker should be empowered to award two or zero but not one.

(*j*) Negative marks should not be given. In Example 8.12 the examiner has decided to award two marks for each correct answer, but has the problem of what to do with a student who lists, say 'Vitamins B, C and K'. It would seem unjust to ignore the incorrect answer, as the student would then receive the same mark as another who had omitted K because he knew it was not water-soluble. In this instance the wording of the question should be changed to 'State whether each of the following vitamins is water-soluble or fat-soluble'. One mark can then be awarded for each correct answer.

(*k*) 'Bonus marks' should not be awarded, as they are likely to be given on a subjective basis. The need for bonus marks is most likely to occur if the question has not been written with the marking scheme in mind so that, for example, five marks are available for four points. The temptation is

## EXAMPLES

### 8.11 *Electrical Craft*

In the figure below an alternating current is passed through two pure inductors L1 and L2. Explain why a voltage will be registered

(a) on V1 (b) on V2

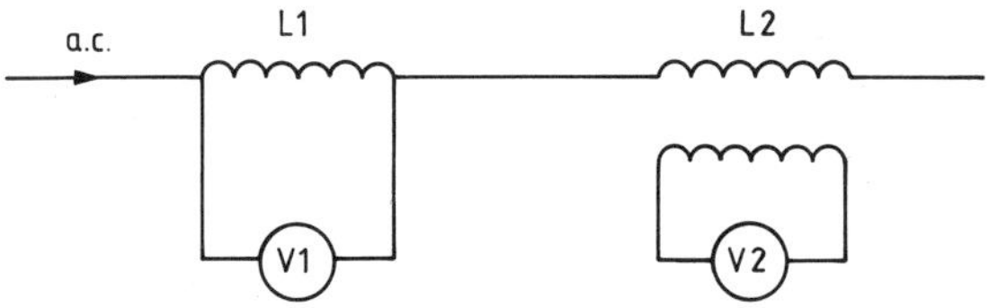


**Marking Scheme**

(a) Alternating current through L1 causes alternating flux which cuts inductor turns and induces voltage (self-inductance) 5

(b) Alternating current through L2 causes alternating flux which cuts second inductor turns and induces voltage (mutual inductance) 5

### 8.12 *Food Technology*

State which of the following vitamins are water-soluble.

(a) A
(b) B
(c) C
(d) D
(e) K

**Marking Scheme**

Vitamins B and C 2 marks each

Deduct 1 mark for each incorrect answer given

then to award the fifth mark for neatness, self-expression or to any student who answers three or four points correctly. It would be much better to limit the marks available for the question to four; if this cannot be done because it is an optional question, the question itself should be revised.

(*l*) There is no need for the total marks for the paper to be 100. Although many people find it easy to think in terms of percentage marks, there is no magic in the figure of 100, and its use can often be a disadvantage, as it does not subdivide easily. It is preferable to use another total which fits the structure of the paper better, e.g. 120 (10 questions at 12 marks, 6 questions at 20 marks) or 150 (10 questions at 15 marks) or 60 (30 question at two marks). A convenient total mark for each structured question is 12, as it can be divided into two, three, four or six according to the structure of the question. If it is really necessary, the total marks for the paper can be converted to percentages, for example so that they may be combined with the marks from another paper, but in general there are disadvantages in combining the marks of two or more papers in this way and each paper's result should normally stand on its own. (This subject is discussed in greater detail in Book 1 of the series.) If it is accepted that the marks for the paper need not total 100, than there is no need to award 'bonus marks' for the paper as a whole to bring the total up to 100.

## The Marking Scheme for Written Questions

The marking of written questions is likely to present more problems than that of calculations because the answers are usually more varied, even if the question is well structured. One- or two-word answers to short questions can give more reliable marking than longer answers.

Points to note in preparing the marking scheme for a written question are:

(*a*) There should be a brief statement of the answer expected. At this stage of preparation, it is not necessary to give a full list of alternative acceptable answers.

(*b*) There should be an indication of the number of points which are expected and for which marks will be awarded — this should, of course, be apparent from the question.

(*c*) Marks should be allocated for such abilities as identification of the problem, workability of the solution and logical presentation of the answer if it is part of the point of the question to assess these abilities, but not otherwise.

Example 8.13 shows the outline answer and marking scheme for a structured question.

## The Marking Scheme for Calculations

An example of a marking scheme for a calculation question is given as Example 8.14. This question was used as Example 6.14 to illustrate the desirability of structuring the calculation and arranging it in the order in which the student needs to tackle it. This makes devising the marking scheme much easier.

Some points to note when preparing the marking scheme for calculations are:

(*a*) The solution should be given in full. This enables both the examiner and the moderators to check that there *is* an answer and that the figures are not unnecessarily complex for the level being examined.

(*b*) The marks awarded for each stage should be shown.

(*c*) Marks for method should be distinguished from marks for accuracy of calculations. In the example given, two marks are awarded at each stage for substituting numbers in the correct formulae (e.g. for stating area of triangle = (24 × 9)/2). At a lower level it would probably be necessary to subdivide this, allowing perhaps one mark for stating the formula

---

### EXAMPLE

**8.13** *Fabrication and Welding Technicians*

(a) What is the function of a suppressor on a tungsten arc gas-shielded welding set? (4 marks)

(b) What is the function of a contactor in a gas-shielded welding circuit? (4 marks)

(c) The following gases are used for gas-shielded metal arc welding. In EACH case state ONE material and the mode of metal transfer for which each gas is most suitable
 (i) argon
 (ii) argon + 15% nitrogen
 (iii) agron + 5% oxygen. (12 marks)

**Marking Scheme**

| | | | |
|---|---|---|---|
| (a) | | A suppressor is fitted to prevent inherent rectification of a.c. current taking place. It suppresses the d.c. component. | 4 |
| (b) | | A contactor is fitted to ensure that the electrode is 'dead' when the set is not in use. | 4 |
| (c) | (i) | Aluminium, nickel or copper | 2 |
| | | Dip, pulse or spray. | 2 |
| | (ii) | Copper | 2 |
| | | Spray | 2 |
| | (iii) | Low carbon or low alloy steels | 2 |
| | | Pulse or spray | 2 |
| | | | 20 |

(base × height)/2 and one mark for substituting the correct figures for the problem given in the question.

(*d*) The relative weighting given to method and accuracy will vary according to the level and purpose of the examination. Frequently method will be rated more highly than accuracy.

---

## EXAMPLE

**8.14** *Mechanical Technicians*

The figure below shows the segment of a circle ABCDA. Calculate:

(a) the distance OD
(b) the area of the triangle ACO
(c) the angle $\theta$
(d) the area of the sector OABCO
(e) the area of the segment ABCDA.

(No marks will be awarded for a solution obtained by measuring a scale drawing.)

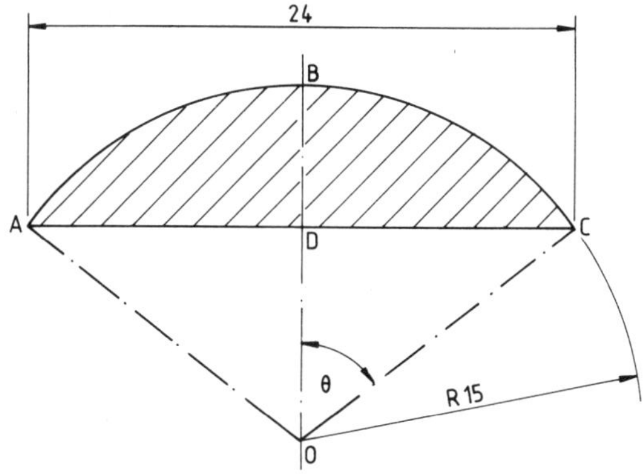


| **Marking Scheme** | | Method | Accuracy |
|---|---|---|---|
| (a) $OD = \sqrt{(15^2 - 12^2)}$ | $= 9$ | 2 | 2 |
| (b) area of triangle ACO | $= \dfrac{24 \times 9}{2}$ | | |
| | $= 108$ | 2 | 2 |
| (c) $\theta = \arcsin\dfrac{12}{15} = 53.13^\circ\ (53^\circ 8')$ | | 2 | 2 |
| (d) area of sector OABCO | | | |
| $= \dfrac{2\,(53.13)}{360} \times \pi \times 15^2$ | | | |
| $= 280.6$ | | 2 | 2 |
| (e) area of segment ABCDA | | | |
| $= 208.6 - 108$ | | | |
| $= 100.6$ | | 2 | 2 |

(*e*) If the main emphasis is on correctness of method, then errors carried forward will only be penalised once — a wrong answer to part (a) will be penalised, but the student will receive full credit for subsequent parts if he has made no other mistakes. This point is more important in the actual marking than in the production of the draft marking scheme at this stage.

(*f*) The marks awarded for correctness of units should be stated if the units are important.

## The Marking Scheme for Sketches and Drawings

(*a*) The marking scheme for sketching and drawing questions will depend upon the purpose of the question. If, as in Examples 8.15 and 8.16, at least part of the point of the question is to test technical understanding, then marks will be awarded mainly for this rather than for accurate drawing. If, as in Example 8.17, accuracy of drawing is important, then the marking scheme will reflect this.

(*b*) The marks should be subdivided as far as possible. Example 8.15 is unsatisfactory because it allows complete freedom for the marker to award part-marks to partially correct answer. Example 8.16 is preferable because the marks are subdivided, so that marking of partly correct answers will be consistent.

(*c*) For drawings which need to be accurate, as Example 8.17, the precise degree of accuracy expected needs to be known to the markers, although this may be settled at the coordinating meeting during marking rather than defined in the initial marking scheme.

---

### EXAMPLE

**8.15** *Electrical Craft*

Make a simple diagram of a single toggle, indicating directions of force and resulting output movement.

**Marking Scheme**

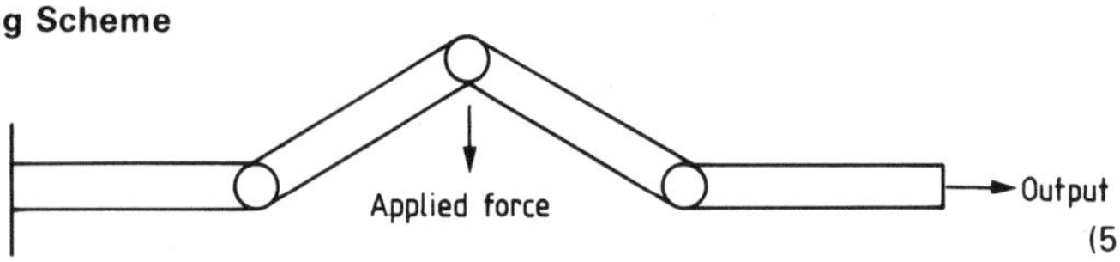


(5 marks)

(*d*) Points which may be included in the marking scheme for a sketching or drawing question are:
inclusion of a stated number of necessary components;
correct relationship between components;
correct proportions;
labelling (if required by the question);
choice of scale;
clarity of presentation.

## EXAMPLE

### 8.16 *Structural and Thick Plate Craft*

The outline below shows a connection on a roof truss. Complete the details of the gusset plate showing position of holes.

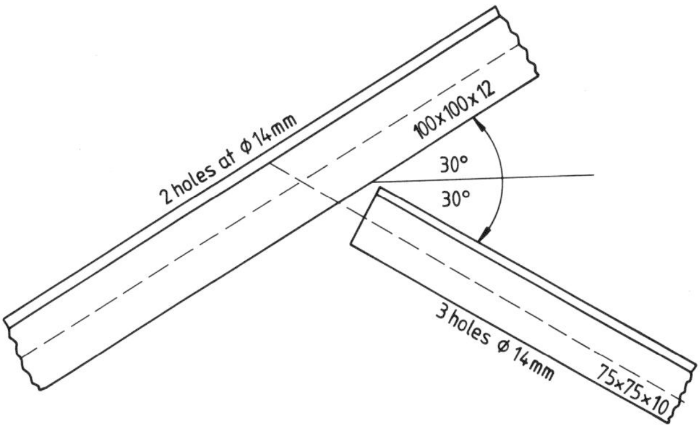


**Marking Scheme**

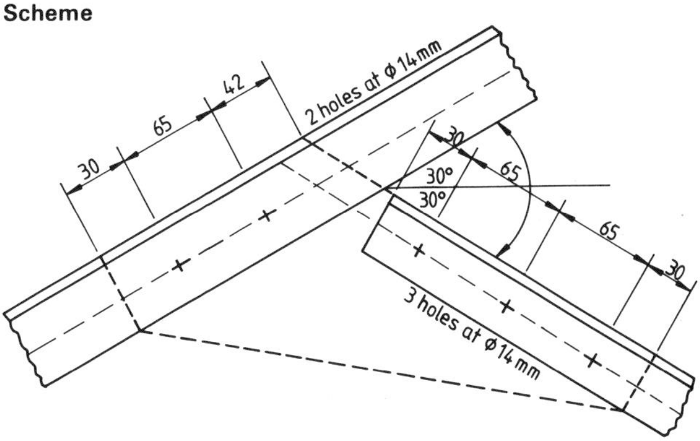


| | |
|---|---|
| Avoidance of back mark intersection, i.e. dim 42 mm | 3 |
| Hole spacing | 2 |
| Gusset plate shape | 1 |
| | 6 |

## EXAMPLE

### 8.17 *Structural and Thick Plate Craft*

The figure below shows an oblique conical hopper fitted to a rectangular duct. The hopper is to be made from two equal pieces. Using the given elevation and half plan, develop a suitable template in the space below.

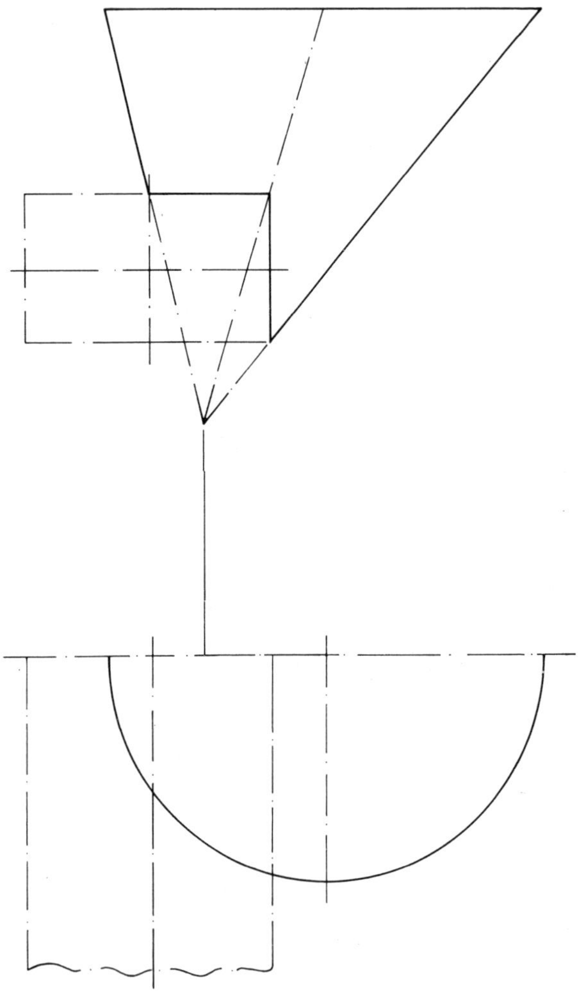

**Marking Scheme**

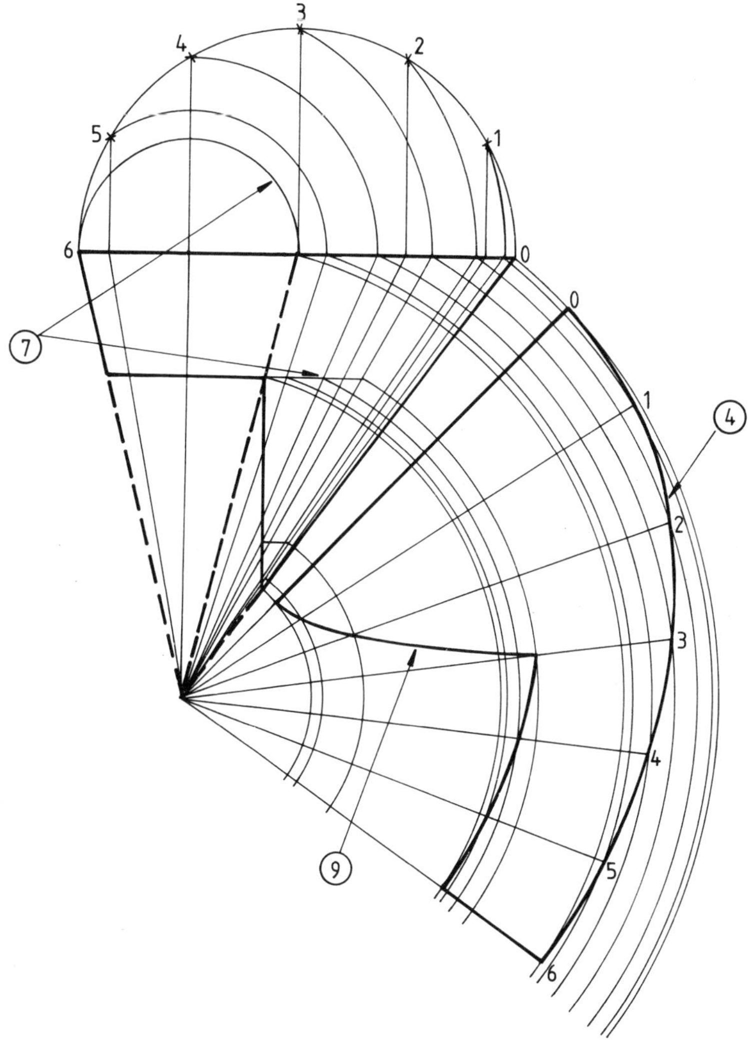


| | |
|---|---|
| True length line construction | 7 |
| Setting out of the developed base curve | 4 |
| Geometry of the cut-off curve | 9 |
| | 20 |

# The Marking Scheme for Phasor Diagrams

Example 8.18 shows the marking scheme for a phasor diagram question. The structuring of this particular question assists marking by ensuring that the students' answers will follow much the same pattern.

For a less structured question the points in the marking scheme might include:

choice of suitable scales;
correct plotting of given information;
additional construction to find other values;
reading off answers;
accuracy of plotting;
associated calculations.

---

## EXAMPLE

**8.18** *Electrical Craft*

The phasor diagrams represent, to a scale of 1 cm = 2 A the currents in two separate circuits. These circuits are now connected in parallel and supplied at 240 V, 50 Hz.

(a) Combine the two phasor diagrams to show the two currents.

(b) With the aid of the phasor diagram find
    (i) the resultant current taken from the supply
    (ii) the overall power factor.

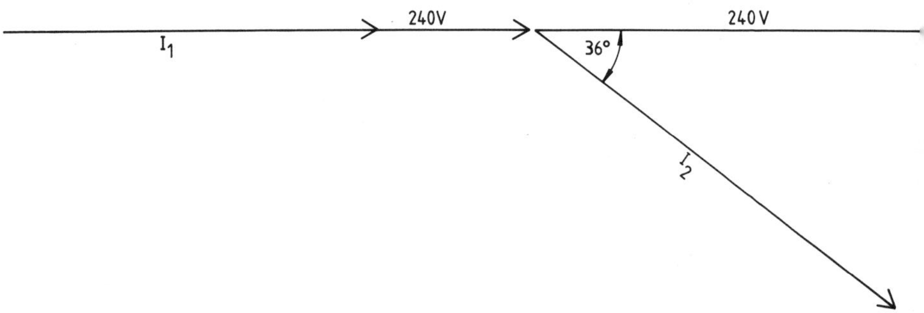

**Marking Scheme**

| | | |
|---|---|---|
| (a) | (a) combining diagrams | 2 |

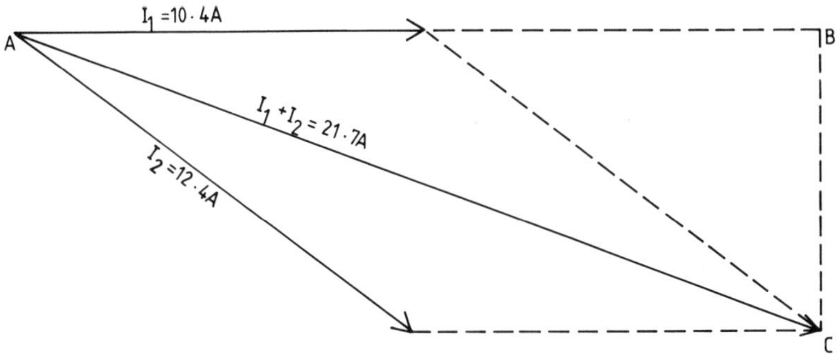


| | | |
|---|---|---|
| (b) (i) $I_1 + I_2 = 21.7$ A | (b) (i) drawing resultant | 2 |
| | scaling current | 2 |
| (ii) power factor $= \frac{AB}{AC}$ | | |
| $= \frac{10.2}{10.85}$ | | 2 |
| $= 0.94$ lagging | | 2 |

OR

power factor = cos < BAC (2)
= cos 20°
= 0.94 lagging (2)

10

## The Marking Scheme for Graphs

Example 8.19 shows the marking scheme for a graphical question. Marking is relatively straightforward for this question because its form ensures that all students are working to the same scale and using the same points on the graph.

For a less structured graph, the points in the marking scheme might include:

---

### EXAMPLE

**8.19** *Electrical Craft*

The figure below shows two sinusoidal waveforms of the same amplitude and frequency, displaced from each other by 90°. On the same axes sketch to the same scale the waveform of the two voltages added together.

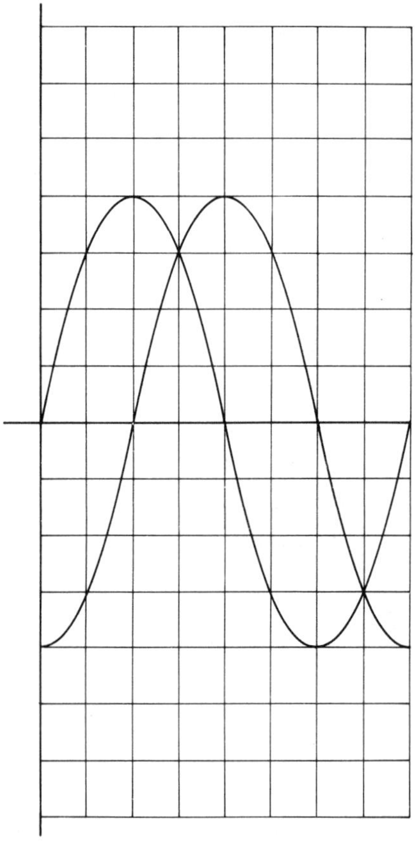

choice of suitable scales;
correct plotting of a stated number of points;
joining points to give a smooth curve;
reading off values as directed by the question.

## APPLICATION

1. Is there a marking scheme for each paper or test with which you are concerned? Is the marking scheme prepared with the draft paper and vetted by a second person?

---

**Marking Scheme**

| | |
|---|---|
| 1 mark for each of 9 points | 9 |
| 1 mark for shape | 1 |
| | 10 |

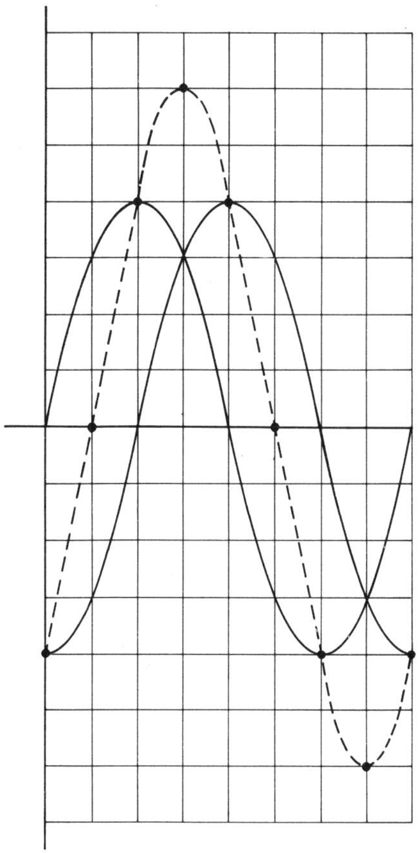

2. Review the marking scheme of one paper with which you are concerned.
   (*a*) Are the marks for each question related to:
   the amount of work involved;
   the difficulty of the question;
   the number of points in the answer?
   (*b*) Does the marking scheme avoid fractional marks, negative marks and bonus marks?

3. Review the marking scheme of each question.
   (*a*) Are marks allocated to everything required by the question? Are any marks awarded to anything not required by the question?
   (*b*) Are any marks awarded for neatness, spelling, English, or similar? If so, is there any evidence that they are awarded in a consistent manner? Are these abilities really required of the student?
   (*c*) Does the marking scheme give the minimum possible scope for subjective judgment by the marker? Has it been tested by a double-marking exercise?
   (*d*) Does the marking scheme show the nature and number of points expected in the answer and the marks allocated to each?
   (*e*) (Calculation questions) Is there a complete solution, with the marks for each stage shown? Are marks for method distinguished from those for accuracy?
   Does the scheme indicate where marks are to be awarded for correctness of units?

4. Revise any marking schemes which do not meet the criteria given in the chapter. Rewrite the questions if this is necessary to ensure reliable marking.

# 9

# Assembling the Question Paper and Writing the Instructions to Students

In the previous three chapters (6—8) we have been concerned with the techniques involved in writing the individual questions and outline marking schemes. In this chapter we look at assembling the questions into a paper and writing the instructions to students.

## Assembling the Paper

When writing the questions the examiner would have been mainly concerned with the content and wording of each and the precision with which it could be marked. He must now stand back a little and consider whether the *combination* of questions is appropriate. The following points need to be considered.

(*a*) The paper must conform to the specification; it must have an appropriate balance of questions on the various syllabus topics and abilities.

(*b*) If the specification is expressed in terms of the type of ability tested (recall, comprehension, application) there should also be an appropriate balance of questions requiring written, drawing and calculation answers, according to the demands of the subject.

(*c*) If the specification is expressed in terms of the form of the answer, then there should also be an appropriate balance of questions testing recall, comprehension and application.

(*d*) The paper as a whole should be appropriate to the student's industrial or commercial background. A single question on the more theoretical aspects of the syllabus or on the fringes of the syllabus may be acceptable, but it would not be acceptable to include several such 'borderline' questions in one paper.

(*e*) The overall standard of the paper should be appropriate to the students' level of ability.

(*f*) One question should not overlap with, or provide the answer to, another.

(*g*) Optional questions should be of equal length and difficulty and should, as far as possible, test similar abilities.

(*h*) Compulsory questions need not be of equal difficulty, and there is probably an advantage in having some easier and some more difficult questions.

(*j*) The arrangement of the questions should be considered, although this will be partly dictated by the space needed for diagrams and charts. If questions are compulsory, it is probably best to begin with one or two easy ones and keep the most difficult until the end. However, students may find it confusing to have to jump from one topic to another, so the middle questions are probably best grouped according to topic.

## Writing the Instructions to Students

The instructions to students, sometimes referred to as the 'rubric', include instructions as to what to do and information on the time allowed and the information and equipment needed or allowed. Rubrics from three different examining bodies are shown in Examples 9.1—9.3.

It is of paramount importance that these instructions are clear — the student will lose some credit for his knowledge if he answers the wrong questions or answers in the wrong manner. Most, if not all, of the decisions concerning these points should have been taken well in advance of the setting of the paper (see Chapter 4). The following is a checklist of points which may need to be included in the question paper heading and instructions — the requirements of individual papers vary and not all points need be included for any one paper.

(*a*) name of examination or course;

(*b*) title of question paper;

(*c*) reference number of question paper (if any);

(*d*) date;

(*e*) time; indicate starting and finishing times (e.g. 2.30—5.00) and also duration of paper in hours (e.g. 2½ hours);

(*f*) stationery required, usually supplied to the student (e.g. 2 sheets of drawing paper);

(*g*) equipment required (e.g. slide rule, calculator, drawing instruments, drawing board and tee square, coloured pencils);

(*h*) reference material supplied (e.g. logarithm tables, data sheets);

(*j*) reference material which the student may bring into the examination;

# EXAMPLES

**9.1** *Motor Vehicle Craft Studies (380)*

PAPER B (380-1-02)
First year
Tuesday 13th June 1978
1000—1130 hours

**Instructions to candidates**
Written answers should be made on lines provided in the question paper.

All sketches and diagrams requested must be made on the question paper.

The following should be provided:

*'Logarithmic and other tables for use at examinations'* by F. Castle, Macmillan & Co. Ltd.

Drawing instruments and mathematical tables may be used.

This paper is in TWO sections, each section contains 50% of the marks.

ALL questions must be answered to obtain full marks.

**9.2** *Scottish Higher National Certificate in Public Administration, Local Government Services*

Monday 29th Novermber 1976 1400—1700 hrs

Answer FIVE questions
Including ONE from Section A
and FOUR from Section B

SECTION A
(All questions carry 28 marks)

SECTION B
(All questions carry 18 marks)

**9.3** *Heating, Ventilating and Air-conditioning Technicians*

Paper 632—1—02 Ventilation and Air-conditioning
Series May—June 1976 Friday 18 June 1976
2 to 4.30 p.m. 2½ hours

You should have the following for this examination
- one answer book
- 'Castle's Logs'
- slide rule
- drawing instruments
- one psychrometric chart (SI units) attached

WRITE YOUR NAME AND CANDIDATE NUMBER CLEARLY ON ANY CHART OR SHEET USED AND PLACE IT INSIDE YOUR ANSWER BOOK BEFORE HANDING IT IN.

Each question is self-contained and no data should be taken from other questions.

Each question carries five marks.

1 Pascal (Pa) = 1 N/m$^2$.

Answer ALL of the following TWENTY questions.

(*k*) any general instructions, e.g. 'calculations to be answered to 3 significant figures', 'take $\pi$ as 22/7' (wherever possible, such information is better given with the question itself);

(*l*) number of questions in the paper;

(*m*) number of questions to be attempted;

(*n*) number of questions to be attempted in each section, where appropriate;

(*o*) information about the time or mark allocation for each section, e.g. 'Each question in Section A carries 4 marks and each question in Section B carries 12 marks' or 'Students are advised to spend not more than 1 hour on Section A';

(*p*) information about the mark allocation for individual questions, e.g. 'All questions carry equal marks' or 'The mark allocation for each question is shown on the paper';

(*q*) any special instructions about answering in the spaces provided or on an attachment to be returned with the answer book.

## APPLICATION

Refer to a question paper with which you are concerned, either in the form in which it was set to students, or as modified by your answers to the questions following Chapters 6—8.

1. Does the paper conform with all the recommendations listed under *Assembling the paper* in the chapter? If not, in what ways should it be modified?

2. Which of the items listed under the heading *Writing the Instructions to students* in the chapter should be included in the rubric for your paper? *ARE* they already included? Rewrite the rubric as necessary.

# 10

# Moderating the Question Paper

## What is Moderating?

Several different terms including *moderating*, *assessing* and *editing*, are used, with some overlap, to describe the process of vetting question papers or individual questions. In this chapter we shall use the term *moderating* to describe the discussion, amendment and approval of the draft question paper, including the individual questions and their marking schemes. This may be done either by a single moderator, or by a group working as a moderating committee. In either case, it should be a two-way process with the examiner, who should be available to clarify his questions and should agree a final version with the moderator(s). The examiner must be prepared to listen and respond to reasoned criticism, and the moderators in turn must be tactful, prepared to make constructive proposals and to justify their observations if necessary.

## Why Moderate?

The aim of the moderation is to improve the question paper's validity and reliability. Validity is improved by obtaining a second opinion as to the paper's appropriateness in subject matter, level and abilities tested. If two lecturers within the college, or two different colleges, are involved in preparing students for the examination, then moderating provides an important check that the examiner is interpreting the syllabus in the same way as the other lecturers.

A moderator outside the college may also be concerned to try to ensure that the standards are roughly comparable with those in other colleges, which set separate papers but gain the same award at the end.

Moderating can improve the reliability of the paper by ensuring that the questions are as clear and well structured as possible, that they are accurate, that they can be marked as reliably as possible and that they do in fact ask what the examiner intended. Sometimes an inspection of the outline solution and marking scheme shows that the moderators interpret the question in a way unforeseen by the examiner; it follows that the students may do the same.

## The Moderating Committee

The moderating 'committee' may be quite an informal gathering and its composition will vary a good deal depending on the examination. The members should, however, include at least one person with knowledge and experience of examination techniques as well as one or more with knowledge of the technology and of the students. A chairman or group leader is needed:

(*a*) to pace the meeting;

(*b*) to ensure that everything is given adequate consideration, but that no time is wasted;

(*c*) to see that contributions from the less vocal members are not overlooked.

It may be helpful to designate someone other than the examiner to act as 'secretary' and keep a record of the agreed amendments. If necessary the 'secretary' should read back the question at the end of the discussion and the examiner should confirm that it accords with his own understanding of what was agreed — this is particularly important if several possible wordings have been suggested and discussed.

Each moderator should 'do his homework' by checking the paper and marking scheme in advance of the meeting and coming prepared with comments and suggestions. This means, of course, that the examiner must have provided the information at least a few days in advance (more if duplication and posting are necessary). It is important that each moderator (whether part of a committee or working as sole moderator) should read the question and formulate his own answer (mentally, if not on paper) *before* he reads the examiner's outline solution. In this way he will check that his own interpretation of the question accords with that of the examiner. He should also work out the answers to numerical and graphical questions and try out drawing questions before looking at the examiner's solutions. This point is illustrated by Example 10.1. At first sight this seems an acceptable question, even if it is a rather silly way of testing the use of simultaneous equations. The examiner has provided a solution, showing that there is one, and has a well-defined marking scheme. However, working out the answer without reference to the examiner's solution would reveal a flaw. The examiner's Equation (1) has $5H$ and $8S$, but the text of the question (presumably as a result of a copying error) states five ham sandwiches and *three* sausage rolls. The answers to the question as written are that one ham sandwich costs £1.75

and one sausage roll costs —£2.10 (minus 210 pence!) The examination candidate who arrived at this answer might be a little worried.

The following three moderating checklists (for the paper as a whole, for each individual question and for each question's marking scheme) are given with little explanation, because the points at issue have already been considered in Chapters 4—9.

## Moderating the Question Paper as a Whole

(*a*) Is the rubric clear and adequate?

(*b*) Are the lists of stationery, equipment and reference material correct, providing all that is necessary, but not specifying unnecessary items? (This must be checked by reference to individual questions.)

(*c*) Will the student have opportunity to use any reference material he is permitted to bring into an 'open-book' examination?

---

### EXAMPLE

**10.1** *Mathematics*

Five ham sandwiches and 3 sausage rolls cost £ 2.45. The cost of 6 ham sandwiches plus 4 sausage rolls is £ 2.10. Find the cost of

(a) 1 ham sandwich

(b) 1 sausage roll.

**Marking Scheme**

**Let** $H$ = ham sandwich and
$S$ = sausage roll

| | | Method | Accuracy |
|---|---|---|---|
| (1) | $5H + 8S = 245$ | | |
| (2) | $6H + 4S = 210$ | | |
| multiply (2) by 2 | $12H + 8S = 420$ | 2 | 1 |
| subtract (1) | $5H + 8S = 245$ | | |
| | $7H = 175$ | | |
| | $H = 25$ | 2 | 1 |
| substitute in (1) | | | |
| | $5H + 8S = 245$ | | |
| | $8S = 245 - 125$ | | |
| | $= 120$ | | |
| | $S = 15$ | 2 | 2 |
| check in (2) | | | |
| | $6H + 4S = 150 + 60$ | | |
| | $= 210$ | 2 | |
| 1 ham sandwich costs 25 p; 1 sausage roll costs 15 p | | 12 | |

(*d*) Are the number and type of questions what the student is expecting? Are they the same as in past examinations or have the students been warned that there is to be a change? (If not, they may be upset.)

(*e*) Does the question paper conform to the specification? Does it test an appropriate range of topics and abilities?

(*f*) Is the overall level of the paper appropriate? Is it similar to that in previous examinations, appropriate for the students and comparable with the papers for other classes or set in other colleges?

(*g*) Is the amount of work appropriate for the time allowed?

(*h*) Is the paper as a whole relevant to the students' work experience?

(*j*) Is the paper sufficiently different from the last one or two papers set?

(*k*) Are all optional questions of equal length and difficulty? Do they test similar abilities?

(*l*) Do the questions overlap or answer one another?

## Moderating each Question

(*a*) Is the question within the syllabus and in accordance with the specification? (It is usually helpful for the examiner to mark the syllabus section on the draft.)

(*b*) Does the question test important and relevant knowledge and abilities?

(*c*) Is the form of answer expected the most appropriate one? Or does the question place too much emphasis on the student's ability to express himself in writing or drawing, at the expense of technical knowledge which ought to be assessed?

(*d*) Is the question of the right standard of difficulty?

(*e*) Is the length of time required for the answer appropriate to the number of marks available and the time allowed for the whole paper?

(*f*) Is the question technically correct and up-to-date?

(*g*) Is there a generally agreed answer to the question?

(*h*) Is the question as well structured as it could be?

(*j*) Does the question indicate the scope, length and form of answer required and the number of points expected?

(*k*) Is the question arranged in the most logical order?

(*l*) Does the question make the most efficient use of the student's examination time? Does it avoid unnecessary repetition?

(*m*) Is the question clear and unambiguous in its wording and diagrams and in the instructions which it gives to students?

(*n*) Is any accompanying diagram correct and complete?

(*o*) Does the question avoid (or, if necessary, explain) any terms or abbreviations which might be unknown to the students?

(*p*) Is the question phrased in correct, grammatical English?

(*q*) Are the symbols, units and abbreviations correct?

(*r*) Does the question supply any data, formulae or other information which the student cannot be expected to memorise? If not, is it available in the works of reference permitted in the examination?

## Moderating the Marking Scheme

(*a*) Does the outline answer represent an appropriate answer to the question as set?

(*b*) Is it technically correct? Are numerical solutions correct?

(*c*) Does the outline answer include everything required by the question and allocate marks for it?

(*d*) Do the outline answer and marking scheme include *only* what is clearly required by the question?

(*e*) Are marks allocated only for the knowledge and abilities required by the question, excluding marks for irrelevant abilities (e.g. neatness, spelling if these are not necessary) and avoiding 'bonus' marks?

(*f*) Do the marks awarded for each answer and part-answer relate to the time required and to the importance of the ability?

(*g*) Is the amount of work appropriate for the time allowed?

(*h*) Is the marking scheme sufficiently broken down, indicating the mark allocation for each point or stage?

(*j*) Does the marking scheme give as little scope as possible for subjective judgment by the marker?

(*k*) Does the suitability of the marking scheme confirm the suitability of the question to which it refers?

(*l*) Do the marks for each part or stage of each question add up to the correct total for the question?

(*m*) Do the marks for each question add up to the indicated total for the paper?

## APPLICATION

1. State the moderating procedure used for a paper with which you are concerned. Does this procedure ensure in practice that the paper is adequately vetted? What changes would improve the procedure?

2. How many people moderate the paper? What expertise does each bring to the task? Do the moderators between them have a knowledge of the subject matter, the course requirements, the students and examination techniques?

3. Use the three 'checklists' given in the chapter to moderate:

   (*a*) the paper you have considered and modified in response to the questions at the end of earlier chapters;

   (*b*) another paper with which you are concerned.

   Note where changes need to be made.

4. Ask a colleague to moderate the same papers and compare his recommendations with yours.

# 11

# Question Paper Layout and Duplication

When the question paper has been discussed with a moderator or moderating committee and amendments agreed, the next stage is to mark up a revised version for printing or (more usually for a college examination) for typing and duplicating. This is something of a chore, but is nevertheless important. Some of the care which has gone into the preparation of the paper will be wasted if it is incorrectly typed or is confusing in its layout. In the stress of the examination students may overlook or misunderstand instructions which are not clear.

The individual lecturer or examiner will not usually have the choice of the method of duplication to be used; if he does have the option, some form of lithographic reproduction using paper 'masters' is to be preferred to the old-style stencils, particularly if there are diagrams.

In preparing the 'copy' for the typist or printer, the first requirement is, of course, that it is clear and legible; clarity may be difficult to achieve if there have been extensive changes during moderation, and it may sometimes be necessary to write out whole questions afresh, or to cut the paper and stick it back together in the new order.

The following are the points to be noted concerning the layout of the paper:

(*a*) There should be an adequate and clear 'rubric', along the lines suggested in Chapter 9.

(*b*) If the paper is divided into sections, each section should be clearly headed, and the instructions concerning it should follow the section heading as well as being given in the rubric to the paper as a whole, e.g. 'Section A—Answer ALL of the following 10 questions'.

(*c*) If the sections are not of equal weighting, this also must be stated both in the paper rubric and in the heading to each section, e.g. 'Each question in this section carries 6 marks'.

(*d*) If questions are not of equal mark value, the marks available for each should be shown in brackets after the question.

(*e*) If each part of a question has a different mark weighting, this also should usually be shown although it is probably not necessary for very short questions.

(*f*) Adequate space should be left between questions, so that they are not confused.

(*g*) Each question should be as compact as possible in its layout, so that its later parts are not overlooked.

(*h*) Questions should not be split between pages. An exception may be made for long structured questions which are compulsory.

(*j*) Diagrams should appear on the same page as the question to which they refer (consistently either above or below the question), or at least on the facing page. If a very large diagram has to be reproduced as an attachment, the reference to it in the question should be in capitals or otherwise emphasised.

(*k*) 'See over' or similar should be typed at the foot of the right-hand page where appropriate.

(*l*) There should be a consistent method of subdividing questions. One possible method is that used for the examples in this book, where the divisions of the question are lettered (*a*), (*b*), (*c*), etc. and subdivisions are numbered (i), (ii), (iii), etc.

(*m*) The number of points expected in the answer should be emphasised, by underlining or the use of capital letters, e.g. 'State THREE methods which . . . and for EACH describe . . .'.

(*n*) Symbols and abbreviations must be correct and in accordance with preferred practice.

(*o*) Typists who are unfamiliar with the technology need to be warned about Greek letters and similar pitfalls. It is not unknown for the Greek capital omega (Ω) to come back from the typist as 'S2'.

(*p*) For a paper which is to printed, there is a British Standard (BS 5261) giving the correct symbols to be used when marking up 'copy' to send to the printer and when checking the proof.

(*q*) Particular care is needed with diagrams. These must be double-checked for accuracy and completeness and for conformity with British Standards.

(*r*) If a diagram is intended to be to scale, the scale must be stated and care taken to ensure that it *is* to that scale, both as drawn and also when reproduced. Processes involving lenses may change the reproduced scale. Those which change the humidity of the paper will certainly change the scale unless careful adjustment is made.

Checking the typescript or proof is also very important. It is helpful to involve a fresh mind at this stage, since the examiner is so familiar with what *ought* to be there that he may fail to notice what is actually there. It is also advisable for a different person to work through any calculations at this stage, to ensure that they are feasible, and that the figures printed are correct.

## 'Question-and-answer' Books

There are some special additional points to be noted in the printing or duplicating of 'question-and-answer books', in which space for the student's answer is left after the question.

(*a*) The instructions to students must state specifically that answers are to be given on the question paper.

(*b*) Sufficient space must be allowed for the answers and the examiner will need to write out or calculate the answers in order to judge the amount of space needed — he should then allow a little extra, as the students may be less economical in their wording or use of space.

(*c*) Sufficient dotted or ruled lines should be provided for written answers. These must be related to the length of answer expected, as the students are likely to interpret them as a guide to what is required.

(*d*) For calculations and drawings adequate blank space must be left.

(*e*) In estimating the space needed for drawings, allowance should be made for any necessary construction lines which fall outside the area of the finished drawing.

(*f*) The typist or printer must be told how much space to leave.

(*g*) Questions may need to be rearranged in order to allow sufficient space for the answer.

(*h*) If axes are provided for graphs, they must be large enough for the answer, as well as for any graph provided as part of the question (see Example 8.19 and marking scheme).

(*j*) Provision must be made on the front page for the student's name and any examination number.

(*k*) It is also helpful to provide a 'mark box' in which the marker can record the mark awarded to each question and the total for the paper.

## APPLICATION

Review the layout of one or more papers with which you are concerned. If possible, consider both a 'question-and-answer' book and a standard paper.

1. Does each conform with all the recommendations given in the chapter?
2. What changes, if any, would you recommend?

PART IV

# Marking and Result Determination

Part III was concerned with the production of the examination. In Part IV we move to the stage at which the examination has been taken by the students and must now be marked and the results decided. Chapters 12 and 13 are concerned with the measures needed to improve reliability of marking whether the marking is done by a single marker (Chapter 12) or by a team (Chapters 12 and 13). Chapter 14 looks at the factors to be taken into account when determining the results of the examination, particularly the pass/fail boundary.

Ideally the results should not be determined until there has been some analysis of the marks for the paper as a whole and for individual questions (see Chapters 15 and 16 in Part V), but it is often necessary to proceed before much, if any, of this work has been done.

# 12

# Operating the Marking Scheme

Chapter 8 described the initial production of the marking scheme before moderating. This chapter is concerned with updating the marking scheme and with the technicalities of marking. It is assumed that the aim is to *mark* the scripts for assessment purposes, not to *correct* for feedback to the students.

## Updating the Marking Scheme

After the question paper has been moderated, the examiner usually needs to revise the marking scheme to take account of the amendments made to the questions during moderation. At this stage he should also expand it to show any alternative acceptable answers and alternative methods of working, e.g. for calculations.

When he actually marks the scripts, the marker will almost certainly find that students have given other answers which are judged acceptable and yet others which are partially correct and can be awarded part-marks. He should therefore keep an up-to-date list of all such answers, and also of any dubious answers which were marked wrong. This is important to ensure consistency of marking, particularly if there are two or more markers, who might otherwise make different decisions about the acceptability of the answers. Even a single marker may be inconsistent with himself if the marking is spread over a period of time, or if, for example, the same examination is set to two groups of students a few weeks apart. If the question is to be banked, then all the information about marking should be banked with it so as to ensure that subsequent groups of students receive the same treatment as the original group — otherwise their performance cannot be reliably compared.

Even if the questions are quite short a separate sheet will probably be needed for each question, in order to give plenty of space for alternative answers. Example 12.1 shows the full marking information for a question. The 'examiner's expected answers' are those which were foreseen by the examiner when the question was set. The 'additional answers' are those which the examiner had not foreseen, but which are judged to be acceptable. (The answer 'helps mother slim' has to be accepted, since the question did not specify advantages to the baby.) The partially correct answers' are those which are either only half true, or which are too vague to be fully acceptable; they are in this instance, judged worthy of half-marks. Under 'wrong answers' it is necessary to list only those answers about which there could be an element of doubt; it is not necessary to record any silly answers which all markers would

---

## EXAMPLE

### 12.1 *Nutrition*

**Question**
State FOUR advantages of breast feeding over bottle feeding.

**Expected Answers**
Any 4 of the following, 2 marks each:

Correct balance of nutrients (lower protein, correct type protein, correct type fat, lower sodium, correct calcium/phosphorus ratio, correct vitamins, correct trace elements in easily absorbed form)
reduced risk of contamination
provision of antibodies
fosters close bond between mother and baby
helps mental growth

**Additional Acceptable Answers**
helps mother slim
reduces risk of gastric upsets
prevents rickets
fat composition changes with growth of baby
easier to digest
less allergy, asthma, eczema
prevents neonatal tetany
cannot be wrongly diluted
always available
less disease, both short and long term

**Partially Correct Answers**
(Awarded 1 mark each)
stimulates blood supply to jaws
prevents heart disease
'nature's way'
makes demand feeding easier
less cost
prevents obesity
prevents cot death

**Wrong Answers – No Marks**
higher protein content
prevents anaemia
high in iron

immediately agree to be wrong. Example 12.2 shows the expected answers and acceptable alternatives for another question.

## Deciding the Importance of Correct Terminology

One problem which may occur quite frequently, particularly in Craft examinations, is that the examiner's answer is expressed in technical language, but the students do not use the same technical terms. It is then necessary to decide whether the use of the correct terminology is important; usually, as in Example 12.3, a correct understanding is more important than the recall of the technical terms. However, if students do not use technical language it may be difficult to decide whether they do, in fact, have the necessary understanding. A question of this type could probably be set much more successfully in multiple-choice form.

## Marking Calculations

Some special points apply to the marking of calculations and in part to graphical answers.

---

### EXAMPLES

**12.2** *Painting and Decorating*

**Question**
State TWO distinctive features of hog's hair which influence the ability of a bristle brush to spread paint evenly.

**Expected Answers**
tapering of hair
barbs along length of hair
curve of hair
flexibility — 2 marks each for any 2

**Additional Acceptable Answers**
split ends
flagged ends

**12.3** *Painting and Decorating*

**Question**
State how the application of gloss paint at a temperature near 0°C would affect the brushing properties of the paint.

**Expected Answer**
increase viscosity of paint — 2 marks

**Alternative Acceptable Answers**
thicken the paint
make it harder to brush

(*a*) Alternative methods of working (e.g. a graphical in place of a calculated solution) should usually be accepted, unless they have been specifically excluded by the wording of the question.

(*b*) A student who has obtained the correct answer but has not shown each stage of his working should be given full marks, unless the question specifically asked that all working be shown. Nothing can be done, of course, for the student who has produced a *wrong* answer with no indication of the method used.

(*c*) An error which is 'carried forward' to later stages of the calculation should be penalised only where it first occurs. If the student has gone on to use the correct method in later stages of the calculation and has correctly applied his initial wrong figure, he should be given the full marks for the later stages.

## Order of Marking

It is generally best to mark the answers of all students to Question 1 together before going on to all the answers to Question 2 etc. This aids the consistency of marking for each question. It also helps to overcome the so-called 'halo effect' which is the tendency for the marker to be unduly influenced by a good answer to the early part of the paper and to mark the remainder more sympathetically; conversely he might mark more harshly a student who produced a poor answer to the first question.

## Technicalities of Marking

The following suggestions are made to help the marker to indicate *clearly* the way in which the marks have been allocated. This will help him, if he needs to look back, and will help a chief examiner or assessor if there is one, to review the marking.

(*a*) Use a different colour from that used by the student.

(*b*) Write the mark awarded to each part-question or point in the answer against that part of the answer — including 0 if applicable

(*c*) Lightly cross through any irrelevant work.

(*d*) Total the marks for the parts of the question and put the total for the question in the margin with a ring round it, e.g. ⑧

(*e*) When entering the mark for each question into any 'box' or other composite record, distinguish between '0' (worthless answer, no marks) and '—' (question not attempted). This distinction is needed if the marks for the questions are to be analysed.

(*f*) Total the scripts at the end of marking. It is not usually necessary to convert marks to a percentage.

(*g*) If the student has attempted more than the required number of questions, discount the poorest one(s).

## Checking the Marking

At the end of the marking it is usually wise to get a second person to check that:

(*a*) everything has been marked, including work on any extra sheets, drawing paper and similar;

(*b*) all question totals are correct and have been recorded in the 'mark box';

(*c*) the total for the paper is correct;

(*d*) the total for the paper has been correctly transferred to any marksheet.

## Impression Marking

The type of marking scheme described in Chapter 8 and in the earlier part of this chapter is the most appropriate for structured or short-answer questions, where the examiner knows fairly well what answers he is expecting and what information or understanding he wishes the students to indicate. This point-by-point marking is termed 'analytical marking'. Very occasionally, usually for essay questions, it may be preferable to use 'impression marking'. This relies on the marker's overall impression of the script, without making any attempt to allocate marks to the various aspects of the answer. The following procedure is used for impression marking.

(*a*) Read quickly through a small sample of scripts to gain an impression of the overall level of response.

(*b*) Read through each script more slowly and allocate it to one of three piles: 'good', 'average', 'poor'.

(*c*) Read through the scripts again, a pile at a time, dividing each pile into smaller sections according to the number of grades to which the students are to be allocated. At this stage some of the original judgments may be revised and some scripts may be moved up or down to another pile.

(*d*) Record the grade for each script.

(*e*) The process should be repeated by a second marker, without knowledge of the grades awarded by the first marker.

(*f*) The final grade is the average of the awards of the two markers.

## APPLICATION

Take the marking scheme and students' answers for one or more questions with which you are concerned. Initially look at a short-answer question.

1. Read through the students' answers and list:
   (*a*) any acceptable answers not on the original marking scheme;
   (*b*) any partially correct answers, with the marks awarded for each;
   (*c*) any answers which were marked wrong but were slightly debatable.
2. Were there any instances where two students were given different marks for the same answers?
3. If possible repeat the exercise looking at answers to the same question(s) marked by a different marker. Were there any discrepancies between markers?
4. In what ways could reliability of marking be improved by:
   (*a*) revisions to the marking schemes;
   (*b*) revisions to the questions themselves?

# 13

# Coordinating the Marking

If there are two or more markers for the same examination paper, special measures are needed to ensure that they all mark to the same standard, as far as possible, and that they all treat like answers in the same way. The measures needed are referred to as *coordinating* the marking.

It is helpful for one marker to be responsible for supervising and coordinating the markers; this person will be referred to in this chapter as the 'chief marker'. Although the chief marker is often the examiner who set the paper, this need not necessarily be so.

Coordination of marking is necessary in national examinations with large numbers of students, but is needed in any situation where there is more than one marker, for example where an examination paper is shared by two or three colleges, with each college's students being marked by their own lecturers.

The procedures usually involved in coordination are as follows.

(*a*) The chief marker provides each marker with a copy of the marking scheme, as amended and amplified after the moderation of the question paper.

(*b*) As soon as the scripts are available, each marker marks (in pencil) 20 or 30 scripts, to get a general impression of the level of response and of the sorts of answers which have been given to each question. He maintains a brief record of the answers not envisaged in the marking scheme (excluding the very silly ones) so that their acceptability may be discussed with the other markers.

(*c*) The markers meet at a 'coordinating meeting' under the chairmanship of the chief marker. They go through the marking scheme, and in the light of their notes on the answers actually given, update it, as described for a single marker in Chapter 12. They then have a full list of:

(i) answers to be accepted and awarded full marks;

(ii) partially correct answers, with the marks to be awarded for each;

(iii) debatable answers which they have decided are too far from the truth to receive any marks.

(*d*) During the next part of the coordinating meeting, each marker marks the same script or scripts (up to six if possible) previously selected and photocopied by the chief marker. The markers do not, of course, know during marking what marks have been awarded to these scripts by their colleagues.

(*e*) The markers then discuss their marking of these trial scripts and identify the reasons for any discrepancies between them.

(*f*) After the meeting the markers proceed individually with their marking. The scripts originally marked in pencil before the coordinating meeting must now be re-marked (in a contrasting colour) in accordance with the updated marking scheme as agreed at the meeting.

(*g*) The chief marker inspects the marking of a sample of scripts from each marker, looking particularly at the scripts near to the pass/fail borderline. The size of the sample inspected varies with the number of students and the number near to the borderline; around 10% of the scripts might be inspected. If necessary, the chief marker asks the individual marker to make amendments to his marking or recommends the use of a higher or lower pass mark for the scripts marked by one or more markers.

(*h*) When all the scripts have been marked and checked, the mean mark and standard deviation can be calculated for each marker and the reasons for any differences betwen them discussed (see Chapters 14 and 15). At this stage, if there prove to be significant differences between the markers, the chief marker may need to inspect further samples of marking or perhaps ask the markers to repeat the exercise of all marking the same few scripts. This can help to establish whether the differences in the levels of marks awarded by the markers are to be attributed to differences in marking standard or to the different level of performance of the students. It may also suggest the size of any adjustment which may need to be made to the pass mark for students marked by 'out-of-line' markers; unfortunately, however, markers are not always consistently easy or severe, and a generally lenient marker may be more severe than average on one or two of the questions in the paper.

It is sometimes found that, over a period of time, one marker marking the same college or group of colleges is consistently more lenient or severe than his colleagues marking other colleges. (This might also happen, for example, if two lecturers at the same college regularly taught and marked the students from different firms or industries.) In such a case it would be informative to interchange the markers for one examination, so that Marker A marked the group usually allocated to Marker B and vice versa. This would show whether Marker A continued to be more severe when marking a different group or whether Group A continued to receive low scores when marked by B or C. Sometimes, of course, more than one factor may be at work in depressing or raising the marks of a group of students.

## APPLICATION

1. List the coordination arrangements for a scheme with which you are concerned (for example a scheme shared with another college). In what ways could the arrangements be improved?

2. Examine a sample of scripts marked by 2 or 3 markers (20 or 30 scripts from each). For each of 2 or 3 questions compile a list of:
   (*a*) correct answers;
   (*b*) partially correct answers, with the marks awarded to each;
   (*c*) incorrect but debatable answers.
   
   Were there any discrepancies between the marks awarded by the different markers?

# 14

# Result Determination

When the scripts have been marked, some analysis should, if possible, be undertaken on the marks for the paper as a whole and for individual questions (see Chapters 15 and 16); the next stage is to determine the results of the students. In this chapter we shall be concerned only with determining the results for a single written paper; the way in which results for several papers or assessments are put together to give a result for the course as a whole is discussed in Book 1 of the series. The main decision to be taken is the *pass mark*, the level above which students qualify for an award, or for credit for the paper, or for promotion to the next stage of the course. It may also be necessary to decide the mark above which students qualify for a *distinction*, *pass with credit*, *pass with merit* or other higher grade of pass; the level at which this is set depends partly upon the policy of the college or of the award-making body for whose validation the results are submitted. If there are two or more markers, it is also necessary to decide whether the same pass and distinction/merit marks are appropriate for each.

The determination of the pass mark cannot be just a matter of 'the pass mark is 50%'. Although the examiner may well set the paper with a pass mark of 50% or 40% in mind, he is unlikely to be able to judge exactly how difficult the paper will prove to be. Consideration of the paper and question analysis may reveal difficulties in the questions which were not foreseen at the time of setting. It is obviously fair that a paper which has proved to be more difficult than average should be balanced by a lower pass mark (and conversely an easier paper should have a higher pass mark). The standard deviation ($\sigma$) also affects the rate of pass (see page 125). (The standard deviation is a measure of the spread of marks; the greater the standard deviation the more widely the marks are spread: see Chapter 15.)

## Norm-referencing and Criterion-referencing

Since there may be differences in the difficulty of an examination from year to year, resulting in differences in the mean and standard deviation of the marks awarded, one approach to result determination is to assume that the differences are *entirely* due to variations in the standard of the paper and that the same percentage of students should pass each year. This is a form of *norm-referencing* (see Book 1 of the series). This approach may well be valid in a large national examination if there is little change in the numbers of students involved or in the level of ability, but is potentially unjust for smaller numbers of students, e.g. in single colleges, where the ability of the class may vary from year to year. If 80% of the class are passed each year, then the less able members of a generally good class will fail, in spite of being of a higher standard than some members of a mediocre class who pass in another year.

The other main approach is *criterion-referencing*, in which the award of a pass is linked to the attainment of certain predetermined objectives or criteria. This sounds attractive, but in practice it is difficult to specify the criteria with sufficient precision to ensure that the scheme can be operated fairly. It is certainly not sufficient to state as a criterion that 'the student must obtain 40% or 50% in the examination', since, as we have seen, examination papers may vary in their difficulty, spread of marks and standard of marking. Nor is it enough to say that 'the student must, in the opinion of the marker, be of acceptable employable standard', as this will not give a consistent standard, particularly over a period of years or if there is more than one marker. Sometimes, for practical skills or lists of facts to be recalled, it may be possible to write precise examination objectives which provide a criterion for assessment, but it is not possible to list all the applications of an item of knowledge which may be expected. Also, a written paper tests only a sample of the syllabus and the sample tested in one examination may well be more difficult than that in another, even if a specification is used.

In practice an examiner is unlikely to use either norm-referencing or criterion-referencing as the sole means of determining the pass mark, but to take into account as many factors as possible.

## The Normal Curve

If the marks obtained by all students for an examination are plotted as a frequency distribution (as described in Chapter 15) or on a graph with the horizontal axis representing marks and the vertical axis representing number of students, then it will usually be found that the distribution has a 'hump' in the middle and flattens out at the ends, showing that most students obtained marks near to the mean, and fewer obtained marks at the extremes. For a large number of students (several hundred or more) it may be found that the distribution, like many distributions from observations in nature, is close to the 'normal distribution' shown in Example 14.1. The normal distribution is mathematically based and there is a fixed relationship between distance from the mean (expressed in number of standard deviations) and percentage of the population; for example 68.26% of the population are within $1\sigma$ (standard deviation) of the mean, above and below, leaving 15.87% at each end of the distribution. The percentage of the population which falls within plus or minus $2\sigma$ of the mean is 95.4.

The normal curve may appear fatter or thinner, taller or shorter, according to the size of the standard deviation and the scale chosen for the graph, but the proportions just quoted remain true. Not all examination distributions correspond closely to the normal curve and the smaller the number of students, the less the likelihood of a close correspondence. Distributions may also be 'skewed', so that the 'hump' does not occur in the middle of the range, i.e. it is not at the mean. Example 14.2 shows a distribution which is negatively skewed, with a higher proportion of the students at the upper end of the

## EXAMPLES

**14.1** *The Normal Distribution*

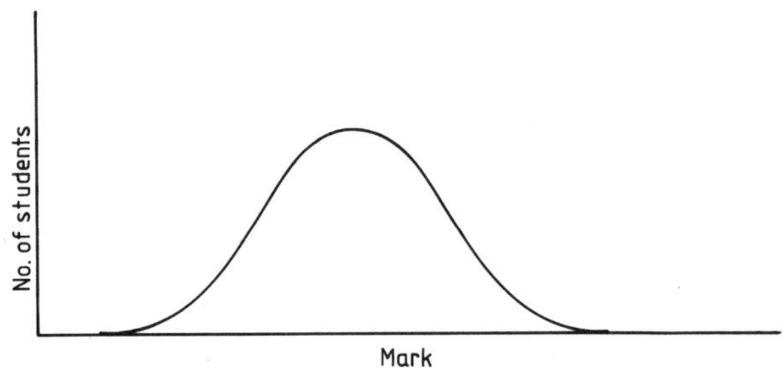


**14.2** *Negatively Skewed Distribution*

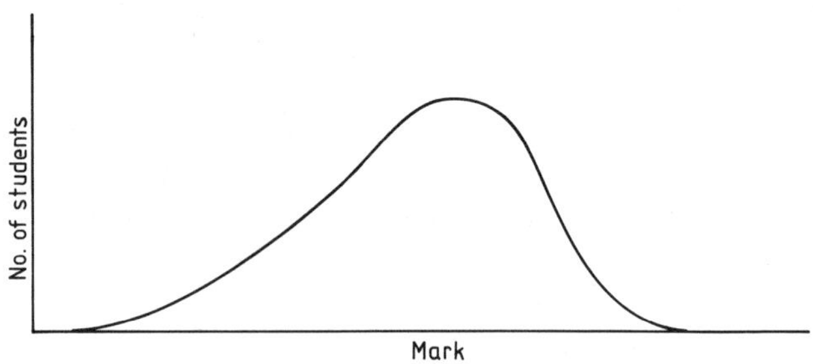

distribution. This might occur if the paper were generally rather too easy. Conversely, a positively skewed distribution would have a higher proportion of students at the lower end of the range.

## The Effect of the Standard Deviation on the Pass Rate

Example 14.3 illustrates the effect of the standard deviation, and also of the mean, on the pass rate, for a given pass mark. Each of the three curves, A, B and C, is a normal distribution of 1000 students. A has a mean of 47 and standard deviation of 10, B has a mean of 50 and standard deviation of 10, C has mean 50, standard deviation 15. A and B, having the same $\sigma$ are the in the same proportions, but A, having a lower mean is displaced three marks to the left. B and C have the same mean, but as C has a higher $\sigma$ it has fewer students near the mean and extends further towards the edges of the graph. It can be seen that there are more C students than B students below 40, so that if the pass mark were 40 for each curve, the pass rate would be lower for C than for

---

**EXAMPLE**

**14.3** *Effect of Standard Deviation*

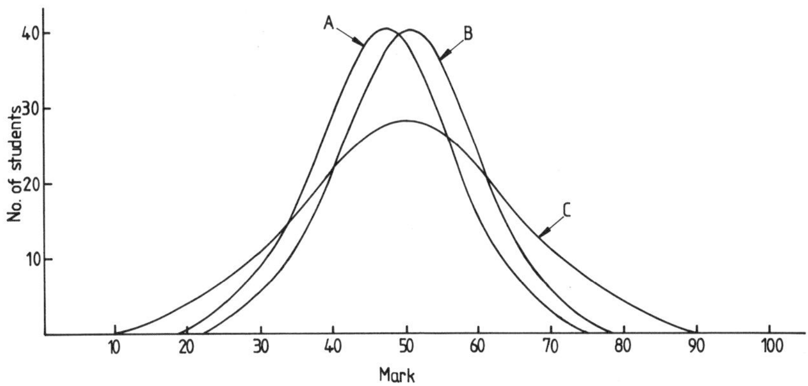


| Curve | Mean | $\sigma$ | % pass at pass mark of 35 | 40 | 45 | % Distn/merit at D/M mark of 60 | 65 | 70 |
|---|---|---|---|---|---|---|---|---|
| A | 47 | 10 | 89 | 76 | 58 | 9.7 | 3.6 | 1.1 |
| B | 50 | 10 | 93 | 84 | 69 | 15.9 | 6.7 | 2.3 |
| C | 50 | 15 | 84 | 75 | 63 | 25.1 | 15.9 | 9.2 |

B. The table below the graph shows that C would have a very slightly lower pass rate (at 40% pass mark) than A, although C has a higher mean. The table also shows that, because C has more students at the top end of the mark range, it would have a higher percentage of distinctions or merits than A or B, whichever of three points were taken as the distinction/merit mark.

If these three curves are taken as representing the results of three papers on the same subject set to the same 1000 students, then it is apparent that the pass marks for the three papers should be adjusted to take account of their different characteristics; otherwise the results of the students would be unduly influenced by the fact that paper A was more difficult than B and that C differentiated better between students of different abilities—the latter point is something which it is difficult for the examiner to foresee very accurately when setting the paper.

The curves might also be taken to illustrate the marking of three markers, although the numbers of students marked by each marker would normally be much less than 1000. If there were good reason to suppose that the differences were due to the idiosyncracies of the markers rather than to the standard of the students, then again, adjustment to the pass marks for two of the three markers would be required in order to avoid injustice.

## Determining the Pass Mark for the Paper

Ultimately, the determination of the pass mark, and the resulting pass rate, must be a matter for the professional judgment of subject experts with a knowledge of the technology, the students, the examination techniques used, the purpose of the test and the uses made of it. The following points should, however, be taken into consideration when making the decision:

(*a*) If the students are appropriately selected for the course, well taught and adequately motivated, it is reasonable to expect that most, if not all, of them will pass the examination. Given these conditions it is not necessary to have a high failure rate in order to maintain a high standard, and a high failure rate *may* indicate faults in the examination rather than in the students.

(*b*) Unless any reason for a change is known, it is reasonable to expect that the percentage pass should remain much the same from year to year. A list of factors which may result in a change is given below (see *f*).

(*c*) If no change in the level of ability of the students is known, it may well be that some change in the standard, level of marking or type of question in the examination has been responsible for any change in the mean mark and standard deviation obtained. A consideration of the paper and question analysis (see Chapters 15 and 16) may help to indicate what these changes might be.

(*d*) One of the best ways of comparing the standard of students in a given year with that of students from previous years or sessions is to compare their performance on questions which have been used before. The marking scheme must, of course, be sufficiently detailed to give reliable marking, and the questions must not have been 'leaked', or become out of date as a result of changes in the technology. If these conditions are fulfilled, the inclusion of at least some banked questions in an examination can give most useful information concerning the relative standards of two or more groups of students.

(*e*) Other information concerning the ability of the students may be available, for example the results of an entry test taken at the beginning of the course, results on an objective test drawn from banked questions, or evidence from coursework and the opinions of lecturers (these last two may not, however, be sufficiently objective to be reliable).

(*f*) Factors which may be connected with a change in the ability or experience of the students and hence a possible change in their success rate are:

- (i) numbers too small to be of consistent standard (in a national examinaton numbers of students below about 200 are regarded as potentially unreliable, but a single college drawing all its 20—30 students for a course from one or two major employers might well find that their standard remained fairly constant from year to year);
- (ii) a marked change in the number of students;
- (iii) a change in the ability of recruits to the industry, due perhaps to the economic environment (the standard of recruit may be higher during a period of generally high unemployment) or to the state of the industry itself;
- (iv) a change in the industrial experience or training of the students;
- (v) a change in the pattern of further education, e.g. from day release to block release;
- (vi) a difference in the criteria used for selecting students for the further education course or, for example, the introduction of a lower level of scheme, taking some of the lower ability students from the existing course;
- (vii) a change in the syllabus or course structure.

## Determining the Pass Mark for Individual Markers

If the paper is marked by two or more markers, it is necessary to consider whether any adjustment needs to be made to the pass mark (and also the distinction/merit mark) for any of the individual markers. If the marking scheme is sufficiently precise and the coordination done with care there should be no need for adjustment; and if the mean marks and standard deviations of all the markers are similar, no further action need be taken.

If, however, despite all these measures, there is a significant difference between the marks awarded by two or more markers, then the possibility of a different marking standard and the possible need for variations in the pass marks should be considered. Example 14.4 shows the sizes of differences between means and standard deviations which are considered statistically significant (at the 95% level of confidence) for given numbers of students. Any differences above these figures should certainly be investigated, and for numbers of students below 50, differences between means of 5% or more and differences between $\sigma$ of 3% or more could deserve further consideration.

If possible, the markers should again be asked to mark a sample of the same scripts, without knowing what marks the other markers have awarded, and the results compared. This will show whether there are genuine differences between the marking standards, and also indicate the size of any adjustment to be made. Differences between the marks awarded by two or more markers may, of course be the result of differences between the students in their

### EXAMPLES

**14.4** *Differences between Means and Standard Deviations*

Sizes of difference which are statistically significant at the 95% level of confidence,

| No. of students in each group | Difference between means | Difference between $\sigma$ |
|---|---|---|
| 200 | 3.34 | 2.36 |
| 100 | 4.74 | 3.34 |
| 50 | 6.7 | 4.7 |
| 20 | 10.5 | 7.4 |

**14.5** *Results on Objective and Constructed-answer Papers*

| Group | Objective paper | | Constructed-answer paper | |
|---|---|---|---|---|
| | Mean | $\sigma$ | Mean | $\sigma$ |
| 1 | 58 | 11 | 46 | 16 |
| 2 | 57 | 11 | 52 | 13 |
| 3 | 65 | 10 | 59 | 13 |

allocations, for example if there are two classes within a college or classes from two colleges taking the same paper but each marked by their own lecturers. In a national examination one marker might have been allocated a group of colleges untypical of the rest of the entry.

Evidence concerning the relative abilities of two or more groups of students may be obtainable from some other source, for example from a multiple-choice paper which they have all taken. Example 14.5 shows the results of three groups of students who have taken both an objective paper and constructed-answer paper, with each group marked by a different marker. The results suggest that there was not much to choose betwen groups 1 and 2 on the abilities tested by the objective paper, so that the difference in their results on the constructed-answer paper may well be due to differences between the markers. On the other hand, Group 3 appears from the objective paper to have a higher level of achievement than Group 2 which may well be the reason for their higher marks on the constructed-answer paper. The objection to this line of reasoning is that the papers should be measuring different abilities (if they are not there is no point in having two papers), so that one should not expect a perfect correlation between them. However, such comparisons can provide further evidence to add to what is available from marking experiments.

## Use of Standard Scales

It may be necessary to convert the marks awarded to marks on a standard scale:

(*a*) if the marks of several papers have to be reported in a uniform manner, so that they are directly comparable;

(*b*) if there are a number of markers, some with adjusted pass marks, and the marks have to be reported in a form in which they are comparable;

(*c*) if the marks from one paper are to be added to, or otherwise combined with, those of another. There are, however, disadvantages in this procedure, unless the papers concerned are testing very similar knowledge and abilities (see Book 1).

It is *not* necessary to convert marks to a standard scale if the results are to be reported simply as pass/fail, as distinction/credit/pass/fail or as merit/pass/fail and not combined with results from other assessment components; once the dividing lines between fail and the various classes of pass have been decided, each student can be allocated to the appropriate class without further adjustment.

Book 1 of this series describes the characteristics of some standard scales (Z score, T score, stanine, percentile and graded mark scale) and describes a procedure for converting 'raw marks' to each.

## Borderline Students

It is generally accepted that the marks awarded in examinations cannot be regarded as accurate to within 1 or 2%. Quite apart from the possibility of errors in marking or adding the marks, there are opportunities for the marker to exercise subjective judgment even in the most highly structured constructed-answer paper and marking scheme and the questions themselves may be less than ideal in precision and relevance. So, when the pass mark has been chosen, the marker, or preferably a second marker, should reexamine the scripts of those students whose marks for the paper are just below the pass mark to ensure that the grading of fail is appropriate. Ideally, the scripts of students just above the pass mark should also be inspected as a further check on the validity and accuracy of the marking, but often time does not permit this.

A reasonable policy would be to reexamine scripts up to half a standard deviation below the pass mark (e.g. six marks below the pass mark if the standard deviation is 12). If, however, the questions are particularly vague, or if the reliability coefficient for the paper has been computed and is below 0.75 (see Chapter 15 and Appendix A), then the scripts reexamined might include those up to 2/3 $\sigma$ below the pass mark.

If the paper is one of several assessment components for the course, the scripts reexamined should include those of students just below the normal 'borderline' range who have passed in the other assessments.

'Reexamination of the scripts' does not, of course, mean automatic elevation to pass, but is a further opportunity to put right any injustices which may have occurred.

APPLICATION

Review the result determination procedures for a paper with which you are concerned.

1. List the factors which were actually taken into consideration when deciding the pass mark the last time the paper was taken. Should any other factors have been considered?

2. Compare the mean marks and standard deviations obtained on three or four occasions when the paper was taken. Were there any differences from exam to exam? If so, what factors could have contributed to the differences for this paper?

3. Were the factors causing the change in the statistics, such as to suggest that a different pass mark should be used on different occasions? Was a different pass mark in fact used?

4. Compare the mean mark and standard deviation (if available) or pass rates of two markers marking the same paper. Were they similar? If not, what factors could have caused the difference in this instance?

5. List the procedures used for borderline students. Are they adequate?

PART V

# Examination and Question Review and Banking

After the examination has been held and the scripts marked, it is desirable to review the performance both of the paper as a whole and of individual questions, preferably before the results are decided and issued. The main purposes of this review are:

(*a*) to assist in deciding the results and ensuring that they are fair (particularly the pass/fail division) by highlighting or suggesting reasons for any unexpected performance of students or questions;
(*b*) to enable marks for any compulsory questions which have proved quite unsatisfactory to be excluded from the determination of results and adjustments to be made to allow for any quite unsatisfactory optional questions;
(*c*) to identify any out-of-line markers if a team of markers is used;
(*d*) to provide information which will be of use if the marks from the paper under consideration are to be combined with marks from any other papers or assessments;
(*e*) to provide information helpful to examiners setting future papers;
(*f*) to enable suitable questions to be banked for reuse.

Review of the paper as a whole and of individual questions is also necessary following pretest, although only reasons (*e*) and (*f*) apply.

The review may take the form of asking, and if possible answering, a number of questions about the performance of the paper as a whole and of individual questions. Some of the relevant information may be obtained by observation or simple counting checks; other information is more conveniently obtained in the form of statistics. The interpretation of the statistics obtained is discussed in Chapter 15 (review of the paper as a whole) and in Chapter 16 (review of individual questions). Methods of calculation are given in the Appendices. Not all the statistical calculations described will be appropriate for all situations; insufficient time may be available for the more tedious calculations or the number of students may be too small for the statistics to be meaningful. In any case statistics should be regarded as a tool rather than as a master; they can give a most valuable indication of the way in which a question paper has performed and may suggest that something has gone wrong, but it usually takes the subject expert, with knowledge of both the subject matter and the students, to determine exactly *what* has gone wrong and what should be done about it.

Chapter 17 looks at the advantages of question banking and the procedures involved.

# 15

# Review of the Question Paper as a Whole

This chapter considers the questions which may be asked to assess the suitability of the question paper as a whole and the way in which it has been answered. The necessary calculations are described in Appendix A.

## 1. Does the Paper Conform to the Specification?

## 2. Are the Questions Relevant and Apparently of Appropriate Standard?

These two questions are, of course, a matter for the subject expert and are a repeat of the checks made at the moderating stage (see Chapter 10).

## 3. Did most Students Complete the Paper in the Time Available?

If the students' lecturer is also their examiner and invigilator, he will know the answer to this question from observation. If someone from outside the

---

**EXAMPLE**

**15.1** *Time taken by Students to Complete Question Paper*

| | Time taken to complete | | | | | |
|---|---|---|---|---|---|---|
| | 1½ hr or less | 1¾ hr | 2 hr | 2¼ hr | 2½ hr | Not finished after 2½ hr |
| No. | 0 | 1 | 8 | 15 | 18 | 8 |
| % | 0 | 2 | 16 | 30 | 36 | 16 |

department is to invigilate, or if the examination is to be taken in one or more outside colleges, then it may be advisable to ask students to indicate in a 'box' at the end of their paper, how long they spent and whether they had time to complete the paper. The numbers of students in each category can then be counted and summarised; the result, for a 2½ hour examination taken by 50 students might be as shown in Example 15.1.

This hypothetical examination paper appears to have been rather too long; slightly less than half the students finished within 2¼ hours and 16% had not finished by the end of the examination period. Normally, at least 90% of students should finish within the time, and if this is not the case, the examiner should consider the possibility of reducing the length of the questions. The time allowed might be increased instead or the number of questions to be answered might be reduced but this would necessitate changes in the specification and advance notice to students and lecturers.

## 4. Did most Students Answer the Required Number of Questions?

Although obviously linked to Question 3, this is not the same question; a student may do all he can within the time allowed, but still not answer the required number of questions because of lack of knowledge. Example 15.2 shows the numbers of questions attempted in an examination in which students were required to answer 15 questions out of 20.

In an examination requiring a smaller number of questions (e.g. five or six) to be answered, it might be expected that 90% of students would attempt the required number. In this case, where the number to be answered is 15, it would be reasonable to expect 90% to answer at least 13. The fact that they did not might be explained by one of the following possibilities:

**EXAMPLE**

**15.2** *Number of Questions Attempted*

| | 16 or more | 15 | 14 | 13 | 12 | 11 | 10 | under 10 | Total |
|---|---|---|---|---|---|---|---|---|---|
| No. of students | 1 | 1 | 2 | 5 | 23 | 38 | 32 | 17 | 119 |
| % students | 1 | 1 | 2 | 4 | 19 | 32 | 27 | 14 | 100 |

(*a*) the time allowed was insufficient for the work to be done (answers to Question 3, concerning the time taken, would help to settle this point);

(*b*) the instructions to students were confusing;

(*c*) students did not take sufficient care to ensure that they answered what was required, perhaps because they were inexperienced examinees, or because they were anyway rather short of time;

(*d*) the questions were unsuitable (too difficult or outside the syllabus), or the students insufficiently knowledgeable, so that they *could* not answer the required 15.

If the paper is divided into sections, it is necessary to make a separate count of this type for each of the sections.

## 5. Was the Overall Level of Performance Satisfactory?

Apart from the subjective impression of the person marking the scripts, which may be misleading and unduly influenced by one or two extreme scripts, the best single indicator of the level of performance on a question paper is the mean (or average) mark obtained by the students who took it (see Appendix A for the method of calculating the mean). The mean mark is expressed first in terms of the maximum mark obtainable for the paper (e.g. 48 out of 80) and then converted to a percentage for ease of interpretation (e.g. 48 out of 80 = 60%). There is a theoretical advantage in having the mean near to the middle of the available mark range (i.e. around 50%), since this allows the students' marks to be spread out equally far on either side of the mean, permitting maximum differentiation between levels of performance. However, a mean below 50% would indicate either rather poor students or a difficult paper; the latter might need to be offset by a pass mark below 40%. In practice, therefore, a good range for the mean is 50—65%. If the mean is outside this range, possible causes might be:

| Mean below 50% | Mean above 65% |
|---|---|
| Students below standard | Students above minimum standard |
| Paper too hard | Paper too easy |
| Marking too severe | Marking too lenient |
| Paper too long | |
| Time allowed insufficient | |

Consideration of the mean alone does not indicate whether the 'fault' lies with the students or with the paper. If the paper is internally set, students' lecturers will have formed an impression of their ability and compared them with those of previous years, but unless such impressions can be supported by comparisons of, for example, performance on identical tasks as part of coursework, they may be too vague or subjective to be of much help. This leads on to the next question.

## 6. Was the Overall Level of Performance Similar to that in Previous Years?

Comparison of the mean with those of previous years will show whether there has been any marked change. If there has been a change, it may be due to one or more of a number of possible factors; these were discussed in Chapter 14 on Result Determination.

## 7. Did the Paper Differentiate between Students?

A good examination paper should differentiate between students of different levels of achievement in the topic being assessed; this is desirable in itself and also helps to ensure a more reliable examination. It should normally be expected, therefore, that the marks awarded will be well spread out across the range of possible marks. There are three ways in which the lecturer or examiner can judge how far this has been achieved:

(*a*) *The range.* The range of marks is expressed in terms of the lowest and highest marks awarded, e.g. 32—80, and is quite easy to discover by inspection of the marked scripts. This will show whether the marker has used the full range of marks available (in the case quoted, he has used only half the available range of 0—100), but will not give an accurate picture of the spread of marks generally because it is based upon only two students. There may be a wide gap between the marks of the best and the second-best or between the worst and the second-worst.

(*b*) *The frequency distribution.* The frequency distribution for an examination paper taken by 52 students and marked out of 100 is shown in Example 15.3. Each student is represented by a stroke against the mark he or she obtained, so that the completed schedule shows the way in which the marks of all the students were distributed. This gives a more complete picture than does the range; in this instance the range is 32—80, but all except the two extreme students were within the range 37—75. The frequency distribution can also show whether the distribution is symmetrical (in this case it is reasonably so) or whether it has a ‘hump’ which is not in the middle.

(*c*) *The standard deviation.* The standard deviation, often represented as $\sigma$ (the Greek letter sigma) or as s.d., is a single figure which indicates the extent to which the marks were spread out — the larger the standard deviation, the more the marks are spread out. The standard deviation may be converted to a percentage for ease of interpretation. A reasonable spread of marks is indicated by a $\sigma$ of at least 10% and preferably 12% or more; the distribution of marks shown in Example 15.3 has a standard deviation of 11.9% which is acceptable. Papers which are largely mathematical in content tend to give higher standard deviations than those requiring descriptive answers, and may have $\sigma$ as high as 20%.

## EXAMPLE

**15.3** *Frequency Distribution Schedule*

| Mark | Tally | Mark | Tally |
|---|---|---|---|
| 80 | / | 49 | // |
| 79 | | 48 | |
| 78 | | 47 | // |
| 77 | | 46 | / |
| 76 | | 45 | |
| 75 | / | 44 | |
| 74 | / | 43 | / |
| 73 | // | 42 | / |
| 72 | / | 41 | /// |
| 71 | / | 40 | // |
| 70 | / | 39 | / |
| 69 | / | 38 | |
| 68 | // | 37 | // |
| 67 | / | 36 | |
| 66 | // | 35 | |
| 65 | | 34 | |
| 64 | // | 33 | |
| 63 | /// | 32 | / |
| 62 | / | Total | 52 |
| 61 | // | | |
| 60 | / | | |
| 59 | // | | |
| 58 | // | | |
| 57 | / | | |
| 56 | // | | |
| 55 | / | | |
| 54 | | | |
| 53 | / | | |
| 52 | | | |
| 51 | // | | |
| 50 | // | | |

Because it is calculated from the marks of all the students, the standard deviation is a better indicator of spread than the range, but the two are of course partly related. An examination taken by 50 students is likely to have a range of marks equal to about 4.5 times the standard deviation; if there are 1000 students, the range is likely to equal about 6.5 times the standard deviation.

A low standard deviation is usually undesirable because it means that the students' marks are all close together, the paper has not differentiated well between the students and the gain or loss of one or two marks (which might be almost accidental) will substantially affect the student's rank order (as compared with other students) and perhaps also his result. Possible reasons for a low standard deviation are that:

(i) the students are genuinely very alike in their level of attainment;
(ii) the paper is either much too easy or much too difficult, so concentrating the marks at one end of the possible range (the mean mark shows whether this is so);
(iii) the marking is either much too lenient or much too severe, with the same results as for (ii);
(iv) the questions are not all 'pulling together' (see Questions 4 and 5 of Chapter 16);
(v) the markers are not using the full range of marks available;
(vi) the marking scheme encourages the award of intermediate marks, blurring the distinction between students (see Question 4 of Chapter 16).

## 8. Was the Examination Sufficiently Reliable?

A truly reliable examination would be one in which the students all received exactly the same result as they would have done if they had taken a different, but comparable, paper on a different occasion and marked by another marker. In practice this is something which cannot be tested because it is not usually practicable to set another examination. Estimates of examination reliability are therefore made on the more limited basis of the examination paper's internal consistency, the extent to which the questions all 'pulled together' to contribute to the total mark. The reliability of an examination is expressed as a correlation (one method of calculating it is to find the correlation between scores on two comparable halves of the paper). The theoretical maximum value is 1.0, which would indicate a perfectly consistent paper in which the best student overall was also the best on each individual question. In practice a value of 0.8 or above is good for a constructed-answer paper; for a single class a lower value of reliability might be accepted. This is partly because the reliability increases with the diversity of ability in the group being tested, so that a paper has a higher reliability coefficient if it is taken by a group of students with a wider range of ability.

If the reliability is low it is necessary to look at individual questions to see where the problem lies. One or two questions with a low discrimination, i.e. a low correlation with the rest of the paper (see Chapter 16), depress the reliability; removing them would improve the statistics for the whole paper, and if they are poor questions this is clearly the best course of action. Sometimes, however, questions with low discrimination are testing important knowledge or abilities rather different from those tested by the rest of the paper; removing them would give an apparent improvement in reliability at the expense of validity. Another means of increasing the reliability is to increase the number of questions, provided of course that the new questions are of the same standard—adding poor questions as 'makeweights' would only make matters worse.

## 9. Were the Marks Awarded by all Markers Comparable?

If two or more markers were involved in marking the students' scripts, then the mean and standard deviation of the marks awarded by each marker should be compared to see whether they are approximately equal. It is desirable to compare the standard deviations as well as the means, because a marker whose mean mark is the same as that of others but whose standard deviation is larger, will have a larger proportion of students below any predetermined pass mark and a larger proportion above any predetermined distinction or merit mark (see Chapter 14 for a fuller explanation of this effect). If there are significant differences in the means or standard deviations, it is necessary to ask whether these result from genuine differences in performance between the students or from differences in the standards of the marking. The significance of differences and possible reasons for them were discussed in Chapter 14.

## 10. Did Markers Award the same Marks to the same Scripts?

If there are some scripts which have been marked by each of the markers, then it is possible to compare the marks awarded. If the number of scripts is small, a comparison of the mean and standard deviation of marks from each marker is of limited value; it is more useful to compare the effects on the total marks of individual students, particularly near to the pass/fail division. A table similar to that given in Example 15.4 may be drawn up, although the number of students involved will usually be much smaller. In this table the figures in each 'cell' represent the number of students whose marks from the two markers fell within the limits shown. Thus, two students were awarded marks in the range 20—24 by both markers, but three who were in this range under Marker A were given marks in the 25—29 range by Marker B (for the same work). More significant, if the pass mark is taken as 40%, is the fact that a total of nine students marked 40 or above by Marker B (three of them in the 45—49 range) were marked below 40 by Marker A, while two students were marked 40—44 by Marker A but below 40 by Marker B. Yet results rather similar to these were obtained from markers whose means and standard deviations on the sample of scripts which both marked differed by only about 2%.

If the results of a double-marking exercise of this type prove unacceptable, then in the short term, the scripts of all students near to the pass/fail division should be remarked before the results of the examination are decided. In the longer term the individual questions and their marking schemes should be scrutinised in an attempt to make the questions more precise and their marking less variable.

## EXAMPLE

**15.4** *Marks awarded to the same scripts by two markers*

| Marker B | Marker A under 20 | 20-24 | 25-29 | 30-34 | 35-39 | 40-44 | 45-49 | 50-54 | 55-59 | 60-64 | 65-69 | 70-74 | 75-79 | 80+ | Total |
|---|---|---|---|---|---|---|---|---|---|---|---|---|---|---|---|
| under 20 | 1 | | | | | | | | | | | | | | 1 |
| 20-24 | 1 | 2 | 1 | | | | | | | | | | | | 4 |
| 25-29 | | 3 | 5 | 1 | | | | | | | | | | | 9 |
| 30-34 | | 1 | 2 | 3 | 1 | | | | | | | | | | 7 |
| 35-39 | | | 1 | 3 | 5 | 2 | | | | | | | | | 11 |
| 40-44 | | | 1 | 1 | 4 | 6 | 1 | | | | | | | | 13 |
| 45-49 | | | | | 3 | 5 | 3 | 1 | | | | | | | 12 |
| 50-54 | | | | | | | 2 | 5 | 1 | 1 | | | | | 9 |
| 55-59 | | | | | | | | 3 | 3 | 2 | | | | | 8 |
| 60-64 | | | | | | | | | | 2 | 1 | 2 | | | 5 |
| 65-69 | | | | | | | | | | 1 | 2 | 3 | 1 | | 7 |
| 70-74 | | | | | | | | | | | | 2 | | 1 | 3 |
| 75-79 | | | | | | | | | | | | 1 | 2 | 2 | 5 |
| 80+ | | | | | | | | | | | | 1 | 2 | 3 | 6 |
| total | 2 | 6 | 10 | 8 | 13 | 13 | 6 | 9 | 4 | 6 | 3 | 9 | 5 | 6 | 100 |

## APPLICATION

1. Investigate performance on a paper with which you are concerned.
   (*a*) Establish the time taken by students to answer the paper.
   (*b*) Find the number of questions answered.
   (*c*) Prepare a frequency distribution and find the range.
   (*d*) Find the mean and standard deviation (see Appendix A).
   (*e*) If appropriate compare the mean and standard deviation of two or more markers.

2. Review the performance of the paper, using the headings given in the chapter. In what ways could the paper be improved?

# 16

# Review of Individual Questions

The suitability of each of the questions in the examination paper may be reviewed under the headings which follow. Methods of calculation of the statistics are given in Appendix B (for compulsory questions) and Appendix C (for optional questions).

## 1. Was the Question Clear, Relevant and Appropriate?

Repeat the checks made at the moderating stage (see Chapter 10) concerning the relevance of the question, its conformity to the syllabus and specification, its clarity, length, technical accuracy and apparent difficulty.

## 2. Was the Question Sufficiently Popular?

This is shown by the *choice index* (see Appendix C for method of calculation) which is simply the percentage of the students taking the paper who chose to attempt the question under consideration. If the question is a *compulsory* one, then the choice index *should* of course be 100. If the choice index for such a question is below about 90 then it will be necessary to consider, by reference to other information, whether the question is too difficult or complex or is outside the syllabus. If, however, the question is at the end of a paper which has already been shown to be too lengthy for the time available, then this is the most likely explanation for its apparent unpopularity.

If the question is an *optional* one, then it will be necessary to compare the choice index obtained with what may be called the *expected choice index*, the figure which would be obtained if all questions were equally popular and if all students attempted the required number of questions; for questions in a six-out-of-ten paper the expected choice index would be 60. A question whose choice index is 1½ times the expected choice index merits further examination to see if it is unduly easy (see 3 below), but may well be acceptable. A question whose choice index is less than 2/3 the expected choice index should be further examined to determine if it is:

(*a*) too difficult;
(*b*) too complex or apparently complex;
(*c*) unclear;
(*d*) outside the syllabus;
(*e*) relevant to only a minority of the students (in this case it may nevertheless be a valid question).

## 3. Was the Question of Appropriate Difficulty?

For a *compulsory* question the difficulty of the question can be assessed by reference to the mean or average mark obtained. The figure used should be the 'corrected mean' in which any students who omitted the question are counted as having scored 0, on the assumption that they did not answer it because they were unable to do so. If, however, the question comes at the end of a long paper, and has a low choice index, reference should also be made to the 'uncorrected' mean, calculated on the marks of only those students who attempted the question.

For a compulsory question a corrected mean in the range 40—85% is to be expected. A question with a mean above 85% is very easy (or else very leniently marked) and is contributing little to the paper's measurement of the students' abilities. There may, however, be good reasons for retaining such a question in future tests, for example if the question is a short-answer one on the safety section of the syllabus.

If the mean mark is below 40 it is necessary to consider whether the question is: (*a*) outside the syllabus; (*b*) testing too high an ability; (*c*) essentially too difficult; (*d*) unclear in its requirements; (*e*) too severely marked.

For an *optional* question reference is made to the uncorrected mean, based only on the marks of those students who attempted the question. By itself, however, the mean will not provide sufficient information because the question may have been chosen by students of above-average or below-average ability. It is therefore necessary to look also at the *mean-total* for the question, which is the average mark *on the paper as a whole* of those students who selected the question under consideration; if the mean-total for a question differs markedly from those of other questions it may be pertinent to ask why.

From the mean and mean-total it is possible to infer the *facility* (see Appendix C); the facility is an estimate of the mean mark which would have been obtained on the question if it had been attempted by students of average ability (as compared with the ability of all students taking the paper). The facility is expressed as a percentage and its value can range, in theory at least, from 0 to 100. Since the questions under consideration are optional they should all have as nearly as possible the same facility which should be within the range 40—60%. Nothing outside this range should be considered satisfactory, but the facility values of questions in any one paper should be much closer than this, ideally all within 5%.

## 4. Did the Question Differentiate between Students?

A good question should differentiate between students of different abilities, and the differentiation will be greatest if the marks awarded are well spread out across the range available. Questions with a wide spread of marks also tend to be more reliably marked than those on which most students were awarded near-average marks; this is because precise questions with clear marking schemes encourage the award of maximum or near-maximum marks to correct answers and of zero to wrong ones, resulting in a wide spread of

---

### EXAMPLE

**16.1** *Distribution of Marks for Example 16.2.*

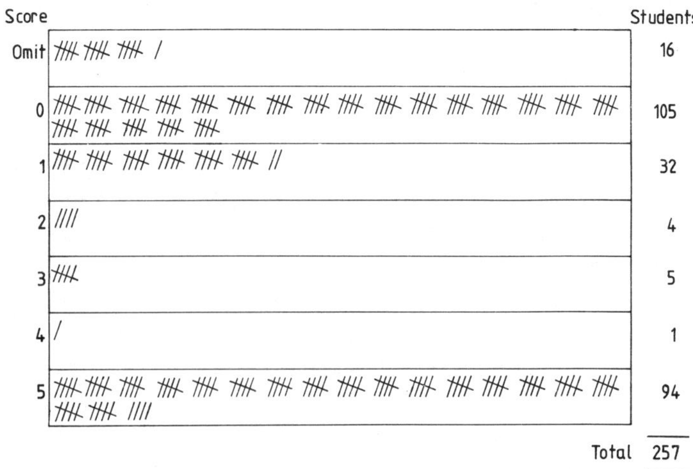

marks for the question; markers are likely to agree in identifying the correct and the incorrect answers to such precise questions, but to disagree in their judgment of whether to award (say) two, three or four marks out of six to a partially correct response to an imprecise question. The spread of marks can be investigated by compiling a frequency distribution for each question similar to that which is suggested for the paper as a whole (see Section 7 (b) of Chapter 15).

Example 16.1 shows the distribution of marks awarded for the compulsory drawing question given in Example 16.2. This question has functioned almost like an objective question with almost all students giving either a correct answer or a completely wrong one. Very few intermediate marks (two, three or four) have been awarded. If the same scripts were marked by another marker, almost identical marking could be expected.

Example 16.3 shows a rather different distribution, that for the compulsory written-answer question in Example 16.4. In this case the distribution is much closer to normal, with 7 as the *mode*, i.e. the most populous score (the mean is 6.5). There are relatively few low marks, but much more use is made of the middle of the range than in Example 16.1.

## EXAMPLE

### 16.2 *Structural and Thick Plate Craft*

The figure below shows the elevation of two right cylinders of equal diameter intersecting a right cone. Using a common central sphere, position the joint lines between the three pieces.

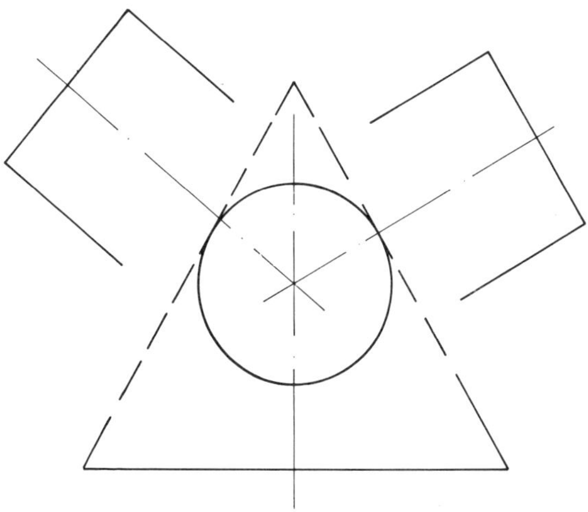

The spread of marks for a question, as for the paper as a whole, may be expressed in a single figure, the standard deviation. The method of calculation is the same as for the whole paper, and again, the standard deviation may be converted to a percentage. However, the percentage value of $\sigma$ expected for a single question is much higher than for the whole paper; values above 20% are to be expected and the theoretical maximum of 50% is more closely approached by an individual question than by the whole paper. The standard

---

## EXAMPLES

**16.3** *Distribution of Marks for Example 16.4*

| Score | | Students |
|---|---|---|
| Omit | //// | 4 |
| 0 | // | 2 |
| 1 | // | 2 |
| 2 | 𝍸 / | 6 |
| 3 | /// | 3 |
| 4 | 𝍸 𝍸 𝍸 𝍸 //// | 24 |
| 5 | 𝍸 𝍸 / | 11 |
| 6 | 𝍸 𝍸 𝍸 𝍸 //// | 24 |
| 7 | 𝍸 𝍸 𝍸 𝍸 𝍸 𝍸 𝍸 𝍸 𝍸 // | 47 |
| 8 | 𝍸 𝍸 𝍸 𝍸 //// | 24 |
| 9 | 𝍸 𝍸 𝍸 𝍸 𝍸 | 25 |
| 10 | 𝍸 𝍸 /// | 13 |
| | Total | 185 |

**16.4** *Carpentry and Joinery*

(a) Explain the basic principles involved in kiln seasoning of wood.

(b) The following types of degrade may occur during the seasoning process. Select ONE of them, identify the effects and give the possible causes.

(i) Case hardening
(ii) Bow
(iii) Twist
(iv) Warp
(v) End shakes.

deviation for the distribution shown in Example 16.1 is 2.3 (46%) and that for Example 16.3 is 2.37 (24%).

It may at first sight seem surprising that the percentage standard deviation for the whole paper is markedly lower than that for each of the questions of which it is composed. The reason is that the questions do not all 'pull together' (in statistical terms they do not correlate perfectly), so that the students who score highest on one question may be average or below average on another. If the rank order of the students were exactly the same on all questions, then the percentage standard deviation for the whole paper would be about the same as those for the individual questions. (The relationship between individual and total-mark standard deviations and correlation is explained in Appendix D of Book 1.)

If the standard deviation of the marks for a question is below the 20% which has been suggested as the minimum desirable, the reason may be that;

(*a*) the question is much too easy or much too difficult (see 3 above);

(*b*) the question is too imprecise;

(*c*) the marker has not used the full range of marks available;

(*d*) the marking scheme encourages the award of intermediate marks rather than the award of full marks to correct answers and zero to incorrect; this in turn may well be the result of imprecision in the question itself.

## 5. Did the Question Measure the same Abilities as the Paper as a Whole?

In most examination papers it may be expected that the individual questions will test generally the same kinds of abilities and knowledge as one another, so that the students who score the highest on any one question should also be among those who score the highest on the paper as a whole. If this is not true of a particular question then the reason may be that the question requires quite different abilities from those required by the rest of the paper; alternatively it may indicate that the question is inherently unsatisfactory, perhaps unclear or misleading in some way, so that the better students are 'put off' and the higher scores are obtained by those who are less knowledgeable. It is very desirable that such questions should be identified and remedied, so the *discrimination index*, which measures the degree of correspondence between marks on the question under consideration and marks on the rest of the paper, is a most useful statistic; it is, however, tedious to calculate (see Appendices B and C).

The discrimination index is in fact a correlation coefficient and the theoretical range for its value is from +1.0 to −1.0 A value of +1.0 would indicate a perfect correlation, where all the better students (as measured by the rest of the paper) scored well on the question under consideration and all the weaker students scored lowest. A discrimination index of −1.0 would indicate the reverse: that all the better students had scored badly on the question and all the weaker students received good marks, a disastrous situation. In practice, neither of these extremes is ever found and a discrimination index above about +0.4 may be considered acceptable; a positive index below +0.4 might be acceptable, but would indicate that the abler students were not in general doing much better than the others on the question. A negative index would indicate that something was definitely amiss and such a question would not normally be accepted without modification.

Possible reasons for a discrimination index which is below +0.4 are that:

(*a*) the question tests knowledge or abilities quite different from those tested by the rest of the paper (the question might in this case be a quite valid one, but it may be arguable whether it should be included in the same paper);

(*b*) the question is either very easy or very difficult, and therefore does not differentiate between students throughout the ability range;

(*c*) the question is of medium difficulty but still does not differentiate between students, i.e. it has a low standard deviation (see 4 above);

(*d*) the question is vague or unclear and fails to prompt the knowledgeable students to reveal what they know;

(*e*) the question is actually inaccurate or misleading;

(*f*) the abler students are looking for a complication or sophistication which is not in the question.

An alternative way of investigating the correspondence between marks on the question under consideration and marks on the rest of the paper is to divide the students into four groups (or quartiles) on the basis of their score on the paper as a whole, those in the upper quartile being those who scored highest on the paper as a whole, those in the second quartile being those who scored next highest and so on. It is then possible to calculate the mean mark of each group on the question under consideration and to plot them graphically. Example 16.5 shows some of the graphs which may result. Graph A shows the best possible result, the question has discriminated throughout the ability range. Graphs B, C and D also indicate quite good questions. Graphs E and F are less satisfactory, but the questions may well be worth retaining. Graphs G, H and I are unsatisfactory and the questions should be discarded or drastically modified.

## Did Answers Receive the same Awards from all Markers?

If two or more markers are involved in the marking, it is useful to compare their marking of individual questions. If they have marked entirely different batches of scripts it is possible to work out separate analysis (calculation of facility and discrimination, for example) for the two batches, but this will not establish whether the causes of any differences lie with the markers or the students. It is much more enlightening to have a sample of scripts (between six and ten would be sufficient), marked by both (or all) markers, who should not, of course, know what marks have been awarded by their colleagues; the results for the paper as a whole and for each question can then be compared.

For two markers the results of the exercise could be shown in a table similar to that used for the results of the paper as a whole (see Chapter 15, Example 15.4). For more than two markers a table might be prepared as shown in

### EXAMPLE

**16.5** *Quartile Means on Individual Questions*

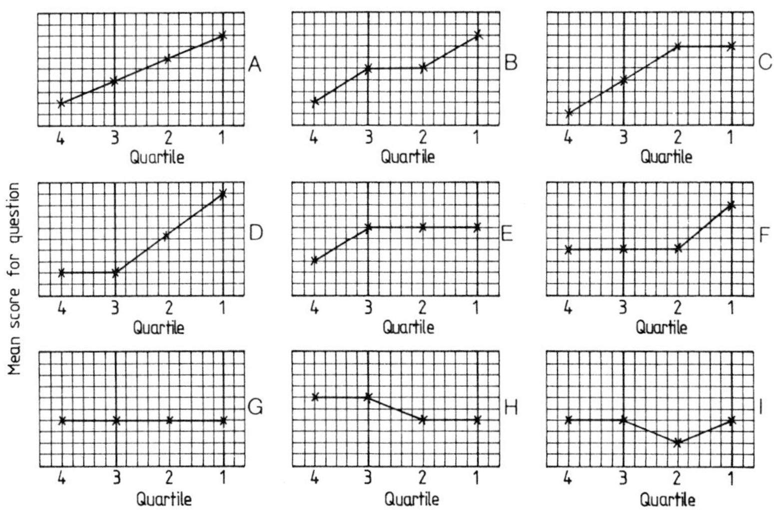

Example 16.6. This table relates to the answers to one question only. Each marker's mark for each answer to this question is shown in the table, with the mean mark and range for each marker and for each student. Quite a wide variation is apparent in this example, with one student (B) receiving marks as far apart as 13 and 18. The means of the marks awarded by the individual markers range from 11.8 (marker 5) to 14.8 (marker 1); this is a difference of 15% of the marks available for the question. The results shown in this example were obtained from markers at the beginning of the coordinating meeting and showed that further discussion and amplification of the marking scheme was required. A question which produced as wide a variation as this after coordination could not be regarded as satisfactory and amendments to the marking scheme would be needed before the question could be banked. If possible, additional measures, such as remarking of all answers and/or revision of the pass/fail boundary would be needed before issue of the results.

## 7. Examples of Analysis

Example 16.7 shows the analysis actually obtained for seven questions, all taken from different examinations. These illustrate the sorts of figures which may be obtained in practice and give instances of those which require further investigation; a major part of such investigation would be the reexamination of the question itself and its marking scheme by subject experts.

Question 1 is rather easy (mean 73) but this is acceptable in a compulsory

---

### EXAMPLE

**16.6** *Comparison of marks awarded by different markers*

Question 8 (base 20 marks)

| Marker | Student A | B | C | D | E | Mean | Range |
|---|---|---|---|---|---|---|---|
| 1 | 15 | 18 | 13 | 15 | 13 | 14.8 | 13–18 |
| 2 | 15 | 16 | 14 | 14 | 14 | 14.6 | 14–16 |
| 3 | 12 | 16 | 13 | 14 | 11 | 13.2 | 11–16 |
| 4 | 17 | 17 | 10 | 12 | 13 | 13.8 | 10–17 |
| 5 | 13 | 13 | 11 | 12 | 10 | 11.8 | 10–13 |
| 6 | 14 | 17 | 14 | 14 | 14 | 14.6 | 14–17 |
| 7 | 12 | 18 | 10 | 14 | 11 | 13.0 | 10–18 |
| 8 | 15 | 16 | 12 | 12 | 14 | 13.8 | 12–16 |
| Mean | 14.1 | 16.4 | 12.1 | 13.4 | 12.5 | | |
| Range | 12-17 | 13-18 | 10-14 | 12-15 | 10-14 | | |

question (note that $EC = 100$). The standard deviation is on the low side but probably not enough to matter, particularly as the question has discriminated adequately. Question 2 was not at all popular and both the standard deviation and the discrimination index are low, so further consideration is required. Question 3 was not popular, and perhaps the students recognised it as a difficult question. With a facility of 30 it was certainly much too difficult to be included in a choice-type paper, and in spite of its good discrimination it would probably be too difficult for inclusion as a compulsory question

---

## EXAMPLE

**16.7** *Analysis of individual questions*

| | Question no. | 1 | 2 | 3 | 4 | 5 | 6 | 7 |
|---|---|---|---|---|---|---|---|---|
| $n$ | number of students actually attempting the question | 97 | 12 | 95 | 150 | 203 | 135 | 145 |
| $C$ | choice index – percentage attempting the question | 100 | 14 | 50 | 97 | 91 | 97 | 56 |
| $EC$ | expected choice index – the percentage who should attempt the question in an ideally balanced paper | 100 | 40 | 75 | 100 | 75 | 100 | 100 |
| $M_Q$ | mean for question (as %) – corrected mean for compulsory questions | 73 | 53 | 34 | 41 | 57 | 67 | 25 |
| $\sigma_Q$ | standard deviation (as %) of marks for the question | 19 | 10 | 15 | 21 | 31 | 45 | 31 |
| $M_{TQ}$ | mean-total (as %) – the mean mark, on the paper as a whole, of the students who attempted the question | 58 | 53 | 51 | 47 | 38 | 55 | 33 |
| $M_T$ | the mean mark (as %) for the whole paper, of *all* students who took it | 58 | 52 | 47 | 47 | 37 | 55 | 31 |
| $\sigma_T$ | the standard deviation (as %) of marks for the whole paper | 16 | 13 | 13 | 13 | 18 | 13 | 17 |
| $F$ | facility value – estimate of the mean mark which would have been obtained if the question were attempted by students of average ability | n/a | 52 | 30 | n/a | 56 | n/a | n/a |
| $D$ | discrimination – correlation between marks on the question and marks on the rest of the paper | 0.46 | 0.31 | 0.58 | 0.20 | 0.63 | 0.46 | 0.38 |

without modification. The students who chose it were of slightly above average ability as judged by the paper as a whole ($M_{TQ}$ is 4% higher than $M_T$) and it is worth considering how far their decision to attempt this very difficult question must have depressed their marks for the paper as a whole. Question 4, although a little difficult, is acceptable in all respects except its discrimination. This particular question was an electrical question appearing in a predominantly mechanical paper for motor vehicle students, which may explain its lack of correlation with the paper as a whole. Question 5 is acceptable, and has discriminated particularly well, but the paper in which it appeared, was in general either too long or too difficult ($M_T$ = 37). Question 6 is acceptable in all respects. Question 7 is unpopular and much too difficult, even for a compulsory question; it appeared in a paper which was also, as a whole, much too difficult.

## APPLICATION

1. Analyse the results of as many as possible of the questions on a paper with which you are concerned. For methods of calculation refer to Appendix B (compulsory questions) or Appendix C (optional questions).

2. Review the performance of each question, using the headings given in the chapter. Identify any unsatisfactory questions. In what ways could they be modified?

3. What assistance do the results of the analysis give for the setting of future papers?

# 17

# Pretesting and Question Banking

*Pretesting* means trying questions out before they are used in an actual examination. Question banking involves retaining the questions with their marking schemes and analysis for reuse in subsequent examinations.

## Why Bank?

As the preceding chapters have shown, a great deal of work usually goes into the production of good examination questions and it is a pity to discard the questions and start all over again after each examination. Questions which have been used once, in a pretest or an actual examination, and modified in the light of results, are likely to be on average better questions (more relevant, more precise, clearer to students, easier to mark accurately) than those being tried for the first time. In most subjects there are some topics or question types which need to be examined fairly often; banking the questions for reuse ensures that all the relevant information on the performance of the questions is available for future use.

Question banking also has the great advantage that it allows accurate comparison of the performance of students over a period of years or of several examinations. Only the reuse of reliable questions allows this accurate comparison. It must, however, be pointed out again that such comparison is meaningless if the marking is unreliable in the first place.

Banking does present some problems. It is important, of course, that the questions are kept secure so that students cannot learn the answers to them without understanding the rest of the subject matter of the course (this is a more significant problem for constructed-answer questions than for multiple-choice questions, of which there are usually far more in one paper). The bank must be reviewed at intervals to ensure that out-of-date questions are excluded, and must be regularly augmented by the production of new questions. The administrative work involved is greater than if a fresh paper were set for each examination.

An alternative procedure is to bank complete papers or tests, but this is only acceptable if the tests are as good as they can be. In the early years of an examination this is unlikely to be so. Banking of complete tests may also provide greater security problems than banking of individual questions. The rest of this chapter will therefore assume that the banking is to be of individual questions.

## Pretesting

There are considerable advantages in pretesting questions, i.e. trying them out under examination conditions in advance of the actual examination. In many circumstances such pretesting is simply not possible, but where it is possible it enables the lecturers or examiners concerned to establish:

(*a*) the suitability of the overall level of the examination;

(*b*) the appropriateness of the time allowance;

(c) the suitability of individual questions;

(*d*) the comparability of questions (very important if the paper allows a choice of questions);

(*e*) the objectivity of the marking scheme (this is only possible if some of the student's scripts can be marked by two different markers and the results compared).

Certain conditions must be fulfilled if the pretest is to be of value:

(*a*) The students attempting the pretest must be similar to, but not of course the same as, the students who will take the actual examination; in practice this is usually achieved by pretesting with a previous class at a similar stage in its course. For example a 'mock' examination might be set to one class to help them prepare for their actual examination and satisfactory questions from the 'mock' examination could be used in the actual examination for a subsequent class or year.

(*b*) The pretest must be taken under examination conditions.

(*c*) The security of the questions must be maintained, although students should have an opportunity to see and attempt a few similar questions as an indication of what they will face in their examination.

(*d*) The numbers of students taking the pretest must be sufficient to give a representative sample of the students who will take the actual examination; for a national examination this usually means around 250 students from several representative colleges; for a local examination much smaller numbers would be acceptable provided that they were representative, e.g. included more than one college if more than one would be involved in the actual examination.

Even a pretest with 20 students could be useful in revealing ambiguities or unsuspected difficulties in the questions, although it would not provide reliable, stable statistics.

After a pretest has been held and marked, the procedures for marking and reviewing the questions are the same as for questions used in an actual examination.

## Procedures for Banking

The following procedures are involved in reviewing and banking pretest and examination questions:

(*a*) Because security of the bank is important, all question papers and pretest papers must be collected after the examination.

(*b*) As much analysis as possible should be obtained for the paper as a whole, and more particularly for individual questions (see Chapters 15 and 16).

(*c*) The questions and their analysis should be reviewed by the examiner and at least one other person — the original moderating committee might well do this.

(*d*) Questions which seem acceptable according to the criteria given in Chapter 16 should be marked for retention.

(*e*) The reviewers should try to determine why other questions have not performed satisfactorily, and should if possible amend them for further trial. Ideally the questions should be pretested again in their amended form before use, but it may be necessary to use them in an actual examination without further pretesting.

(*f*) Questions which are unsatisfactory and appear impossible to improve should be rejected.

(*g*) The accepted questions are typed or stuck on to sheets of paper or card, one question per sheet, with all relevant information (see below).

(*h*) The bank sheets or cards are arranged in order of syllabus section or of specification reference.

(*j*) When a fresh examination paper is needed a set of suitable questions is selected from the bank (see 'Compiling a Paper' below).

(*k*) After each use of the question, the analysis obtained is added to the bank record.

(*l*) The size of the bank is gradually increased, either by pretesting new questions or by including some untried questions in each examination.

(*m*) The contents of the bank must be reviewed at intervals to remove questions which have become out-of-date as a result of technological or other change.

(*n*) An attempt should be made to keep the number of questions in each section of the bank (e.g. for each syllabus topic) proportional to the number required in each paper, according to the specification.

## Information Required for Each Question

Example 17.1 gives a possible layout for a bank card. The following information is required for each question:

(*a*) course and question paper title;

---

### EXAMPLE

**17.1** *Electrical and Electronic Craft Studies Part III*

Paper: Electrical Control
Syllabus section:

Bank number: 3
Type of answer: sketching

QUESTION
Draw a three-input AND gate using simple switches.

MARKING SCHEME

| | |
|---|---|
| Switch symbol | 1 |
| Arrangement | 3 |
| | 4 |

USE AND ANALYSIS

| Date | Jun 1973 |
|---|---|
| $n$ | 135 |
| $C$ | 97 |
| EC | 100 |
| $M_Q$ | 2.6 |
| (as %) | 65 |
| $\sigma_Q$ | 1.8 |
| (as %) | 46 |
| $M_T$ | 55.3 |
| D | 0.46 |

(*b*) serial number of the question in the bank;

(*c*) syllabus section or specification reference;

(*d*) type of ability tested or type of answer required, according to the form of the specification used;

(*e*) the text of the question;

(*f*) solution and marking scheme;

(*g*) date(s) of examination(s) in which the question was used;

(*h*) analysis for each use (see Chapter 16 for explanation of analysis):

$n$ number of students attempting the question
$C$ Choice index
$EC$ Expected choice index
$M_Q$ Mean mark (corrected for omits in the case of compulsory questions) both 'raw' and as a percentage
$\sigma_Q$ standard deviation (corrected for omits for compulsory questions) both 'raw' and as percentage
$M_{TQ}$ Mean-total (optional questions only)
$M_T$ Mean for paper as a whole
$F$ Facility (optional questions only)
$D$ Discrimination;

(*j*) any relevant comments from the markers or from other lecturers who were not involved in the setting and marking;

(*k*) if the question is one which has been amended after first use, it is helpful to retain a copy of the original version and its analysis — for example on the back of the bank card.

## Compiling a Paper from Banked Questions

The following points should be borne in mind when compiling a question paper from banked questions:

(*a*) The paper must conform to the specification.

(*b*) The questions chosen must not overlap in content, or answer one another.

(*c*) The questions chosen should give a predicted mean mark for the paper equivalent to 50—65% (see Appendix D for method of calculating this).

(*d*) For compulsory questions, there may be a range of difficult and easy questions, possibly including one or two quite easy questions at the beginning of the paper, but usually all with mean marks in the range 40—85%.

(*e*) For optional questions the Facilities of the questions chosen should be as nearly identical as possible.

(*f*) The discriminations of the questions should average above +0.4.

(*g*) There should not be too many questions used in the most recent examinations or used many times over.

It is usually wise to begin compilation with the bank sections for which there are fewest questions. The available choice of questions in these sections may limit the choices for other sections. For example, avoiding questions recently used, might make it necessary to choose rather difficult questions from one section, in which case it would be necessary to choose the easier questions from another section (assuming a compulsory paper).

## Estimating the Statistics for a Compiled Paper

For a papers containing only compulsory questions it is possible to estimate in advance the mean mark and standard deviation which are likely to be obtained if the paper is compiled from banked questions. Appendix D shows the calculations required. If the results actually obtained differ from those predicted, it can be assumed that the difference is due to differences in the students (or possibly the standard of marking), not to differences in the standard of the questions.

For papers including optional questions the predictions are very much more difficult, because it is impossible to predict the choice pattern which will be obtained. A question which was attempted by 60% of students in one paper may well attract a different percentage if it is put into a different paper with other questions around it. If, as should be the case, the questions are all of equal facility, the mean mark for the paper can be predicted (see Appendix E), but, unless the question discriminations are also very similar in value, the standard deviation cannot be estimated reliably.

APPLICATION

1. Review the banking arrangements for a paper with which you are concerned.
   (*a*) Is all necessary information banked with the questions (syllabus section, ability tested, solution, marking scheme, dates of use)?
   (*b*) What analysis is banked with the questions? Could more be made available?
   (*c*) Does the bank contain an appropriate balance of questions for different syllabus sections and abilities?

(*d*) Does the bank contain any out-of-date questions or any questions with poor analysis?

2. Review the arrangements for a paper with which you are concerned which does not have a bank.

   (*a*) What extra work would be needed in order to set up a bank?

   (*b*) What work would be saved in the future if a bank of questions were available?

   (*c*) In what ways would the use of a banking system improve the examination's validity, reliability and efficiency?

PART VI

# Appendices

The appendices explain, with worked examples, the calculations required for analysis of the paper as a whole (Appendix A) and of individual compulsory and optional questions (Appendices B and C) and for predicting results from papers compiled from banked questions (Appendices D and E). Appendix F lists, for ease of reference, all the symbols used in the calculations.

Although some of the simpler calculations can be done manually, most require the use of at least a basic electronic calculator. This reduces the work involved and also makes it unnecessary to use the approximate methods which used to be recommended for some calculations. The calculator chosen should have a memory and a square root key. Statistical calculators are now available preprogrammed to calculate mean and standard deviation and sometimes correlation as well. These reduce the amount of work very considerably, but they may have severe limitations in the number of items of data that they can handle in one calculation. Such calculators may be preprogrammed to use $(n - 1)$ in place of $n$ in standard deviation calculations, giving a larger result where the number of students is small.

The following appendices give the calculations in some detail. Most readers using an electronic calculator will find that it is not necessary to write down all the intermediate stages of the working. However, it is wise to check at the end that the answer obtained is a realistic one, as it is easy to make mistakes when keying in the data.

# A

# Calculation of Analysis for the Paper as a Whole

This Appendix explains the calculations involved in the analysis of the paper as a whole. The interpretation of the statistics was considered in Chapter 15.

## Frequency Distribution

A frequency distribution is useful in itself, because it gives an impression of the way in which the students' marks have been distributed (Section 7 (b) of Chapter 15), and is also a necessary first stage in the calculation of the mean and standard deviation if a preprogrammed statistical calculator is not available. The frequency distribution for the whole paper is prepared from the students' total marks, which should *not* be converted to a percentage if the paper has been marked out of a base other than 100. The scripts are examined and for each script a stroke ( / ) is placed against the appropriate figure in a preprepared table to show the total mark received. The fifth occurrence of a mark is recorded by putting a diagonal across the preceding four strokes to form a 'gate' (𝍸) and the tenth by a diagonal in the opposite direction (𝍸 𝍸). A neatly completed frequency distribution can be a useful tool. An example of a frequency distribution was given as Example 15.3 and is repeated in the 'mark' and 'tally' columns of Example A1.

## Mean

The formula for the mean for the paper as a whole, $M_T$, is

$$M_T = \frac{\Sigma x_T}{n_T}$$ where

## EXAMPLE

### A1 *Frequency Distribution*

| 1 | 2 | 3 | 4 | 5 |
|---|---|---|---|---|
| Mark $x$ | Tally $f$ | $fx_T$ | $x_T^2$ | $fx_T^2$ |
| 80 | / | 80 | 6400 | 6400 |
| 75 | / | 75 | 5625 | 5625 |
| 74 | / | 74 | 5476 | 5476 |
| 73 | // | 146 | 5329 | 10 658 |
| 72 | / | 72 | 5184 | 5184 |
| 71 | / | 71 | 5041 | 5041 |
| 70 | / | 70 | 4900 | 4900 |
| 69 | / | 69 | etc | 4761 |
| 68 | // | 136 | | 9248 |
| 67 | / | 67 | | 4489 |
| 66 | // | 132 | | 8712 |
| 65 | | | | |
| 64 | // | 128 | | 8192 |
| 63 | /// | 189 | | 11 907 |
| 62 | / | 62 | | 3844 |
| 61 | // | 122 | | 7442 |
| 60 | / | 60 | | 3600 |
| 59 | // | 118 | | 6962 |
| 58 | // | 116 | | 6728 |
| 57 | / | 57 | | 3249 |
| 56 | // | 112 | | 6272 |
| 55 | / | 55 | | 3025 |
| 54 | | | | |
| 53 | / | 53 | | 2809 |
| 52 | | | | |
| 51 | // | 102 | | 5202 |
| 50 | // | 100 | | 5000 |
| 49 | // | 98 | | 4802 |
| 48 | | | | |
| 47 | // | 94 | | 4418 |
| 46 | / | 46 | | 2116 |
| 45 | | | | |
| 44 | | | | |
| 43 | / | 43 | | 1849 |
| 42 | / | 42 | | 1764 |
| 41 | /// | 123 | | 5043 |
| 40 | // | 80 | | 3200 |
| 39 | / | 39 | | 1521 |
| 38 | | | | |
| 37 | // | 74 | | 2738 |
| 32 | / | 32 | | 1024 |
| Total | 52 | 2937 | | 173201 |

$\Sigma x_T$ is the sum of the marks obtained for the paper as a whole,
$n_T$ is the number of students.

$\Sigma$, the Greek capital letter sigma, means 'the sum of'. In this instance $x_T$ is the mark of any one student on the paper as a whole and $\Sigma x_T$ is the sum (or total) of the marks of all students. For a small number of students simply add the marks obtained and then divide by the number of students.

For a larger number, it is helpful to use the frequency distribution and make up an $fx_T$ column as shown in Example Al, where $f$ means frequency (number of students scoring the mark shown) and $x_T$ means mark. $fx_T$ is therefore the mark times the number of students who scored it; for example, 2 students scored 73, so their combined mark is $73 \times 2 = 146$. When the $fx_T$ column has been completed, it is added to give $\Sigma fx_T$. The mean, $M_T$ is then calculated from

$$M_T = \frac{\Sigma fx_T}{n_T}$$

For Example A1, substituting in the formula gives:

$$M_T = \frac{2937}{52} = 56.48$$

In this case this maximum mark is 100, so the result of the calculation is a percentage. If the maximum mark is some other figure, it is often helpful to convert the mean to a percentage for ease of interpretation. This is done by applying the formula

$$\text{mean (\%)} = \frac{M_T \times 100}{b_T}$$ where

$M_T$ is the mean as calculated above,
$b_T$ is the base (the maximum mark obtainable).

If, for example, the maximum possible mark is 120 and the mean is 48, the percentage mean will be

$$\frac{48 \times 100}{120} = 40\%$$

## Standard Deviation

A formula* for the standard deviation $\sigma_T$ is

$$\sigma_T = \sqrt{\frac{\Sigma x_T^2 - n_T M_T^2}{n_T}}$$ where

$x_T^2$ is the square of each individual mark,
$\Sigma x_T^2$ is the sum of these squares,
$n_T$ is the number of students,
$M_T$ is the mean.

Working from a frequency distribution, as in Example A1, calculate the square of each mark (e.g. $80^2 = 6400$) and then the $fx_T^2$ (the square of the mark times the number of students obtaining that mark), e.g. $73^2 = 5329$ and two students scored 73, so for that mark $fx_T^2 = 5329 \times 2 = 10658$. The $x_T^2$ column has not been completed in full, because $fx_T^2$ can be calculated in one operation on most calculators and it is not necessary to write down the intermediate value. Indeed, on most calculators, it should be possible to enter each $fx_T^2$ value into an accumulating memory, so that there is no need to write down all the $fx_T^2$ values obtained.

When the $fx_T^2$ column is complete, add the figures in the column (or read the calculator memory) in order to obtain $\Sigma fx_T^2$ (= $\Sigma x_T^2$), then substitute in the formula. For Example A1:

---

*The formula for the standard deviation given above is mathematically identical to the more generally quoted formula which is

$$\sigma_T = \sqrt{\frac{\Sigma d^2}{n_T}}$$ where

$d$ is the difference between each mark and the mean,
$\Sigma d^2$ is the sum of the squares of these differences,
$n_T$ is the number of students.

Using this more general formula has the advantage that smaller numbers are involved, but the disadvantages that:

(*a*) an extra stage is involved — it is necessary to find the difference between each mark and the mean before proceeding with the squaring;

(*b*) if the mean is not a whole number, it is necessary either to round to a whole number (with a loss of accuracy) or to work with figures expressed to one decimal place, which is at least as awkward as using larger figures;

(*c*) the sum of squares $\Sigma x_T^2$ as distinct from the sum of squares of differences may be required subsequently, e.g. if it desired to combine two standard deviations (see below). If necessary, however, $\Sigma x_T^2$ can be obtained by adding $n_T M_T^2$ to $\Sigma d^2$.

$$\sigma_T = \sqrt{\frac{\Sigma x_T^2 - n_T M_T^2}{n_T}}$$

$$= \sqrt{\frac{173201 - 52(56.48)^2}{52}}$$

$$= 11.87$$

Like the mean, the standard deviation may be converted to a percentage, if necessary, for case of interpretation, using the formula

$$\text{percentage standard deviation} = \frac{\sigma_T \times 100}{b_T}$$ where

$\sigma_T$ is the standard deviation as calculated above,
$b_T$ is the base (the maximum mark obtainable) for the paper.

For example, if the base is 80 and the standard deviation 12, the percentage standard deviation will be

$$\frac{12 \times 100}{80} = 15\%$$

## Finding the Overall Mean and Standard Deviation for two or more Sets of Marks

Sometimes it is necessary to find the overall mean and standard deviation for two or more sets of marks whose figures are known; for example, if two or more markers have marked different sets of scripts in an examination and the $M$ and $\sigma$ for each marker have been calculated, the overall $M_T$ and $\sigma_T$ for all students may be required. The formulae required are the same as for calculating the $M$ and $\sigma$ for each set, viz.

$$M_T = \frac{\Sigma x_T}{n_T}$$

$$\sigma_T = \sqrt{\frac{\Sigma x_T^2 - n_T M_T^2}{n_T}}$$ where

$M_T$ is the overall mean,
$\sigma_T$ is the overall standard deviation,
$n_T$ is the total number of students,
$\Sigma x_T$ is the sum of marks of all students (from both or all batches),
$\Sigma x_T^2$ is the sum of squares of marks of all students (from both or all batches).

If the sum of marks and sum of squares for each batch are known, then it is easy to combine them to give the overall figures, as in this example of an examination taken by two classes (Example A2).

Substituting in the formula gives:

$$M_T = \frac{\Sigma x_T}{n_T} = \frac{2370}{39} = 60.77$$

$$\sigma_T = \sqrt{\frac{\Sigma x_T^2 - n_T M_T^2}{n_T}} = \sqrt{\frac{153560 - 39(60.77)^2}{39}} = 15.63$$

If the sum marks and sum squares for each batch are *not* known, perhaps because a preprogrammed calculator has been used to find $M$ and $\sigma$, then it is necessary to work backwards from the $M$ and $\sigma$ to find them. Example A3 shows such a situation, again with two classes who have taken the same examination.

## EXAMPLES

**A2** *Calculating Overall Mean and Standard Deviation for two classes*

| Class | No. of students | Sum marks | Mean | Sum squares | Standard deviation |
|---|---|---|---|---|---|
| 1 | 21 | 1193 | 56.81 | 73892 | 17.07 |
| 2 | 18 | 1177 | 65.39 | 79668 | 12.25 |
| Total | 39 (= $n_T$) | 2370 (= $\Sigma x_T$) | | 153560 (= $\Sigma x_T^2$) | |

**A3** *Mean and Standard Deviation for two Classes*

| Class | No. of students | Sum marks | Mean | Sum squares | Standard deviation |
|---|---|---|---|---|---|
| 1 | 19 | | 48.6 | | 13.1 |
| 2 | 15 | | 55.1 | | 15.2 |
| Total | 34 | | | | |

Using this information, the sum marks for each class ($\Sigma x$) are found from

$$\Sigma x = nM$$

So, for Class 1 $\quad \Sigma x = 19 \times 48.6$

$$= 923$$

for Class 2 $\quad \Sigma x = 15 \times 55.1$

$$= 827$$

The sum squares for each class ($\Sigma x^2$) are found from

$$\Sigma x^2 = n(M^2 + \sigma^2)$$

So, for Class 1 $\quad \Sigma x^2 = 19(48.6^2 + 13.1^2)$

$$= 48138$$

for Class 2 $\quad \Sigma x^2 = 15(55.1^2 + 15.2^2)$

$$= 49006$$

These values can now be inserted in the table, as shown in Example A4.

The final stage is to substitute in the formulae.

Overall mean

$$M_T = \frac{\Sigma x_T}{n_T} = \frac{1750}{34} = 51.47$$

Overall standard deviation

$$\sigma_T = \sqrt{\frac{\Sigma x_T{}^2 - n_T\, M_T{}^2}{n_T}} = \sqrt{\frac{97144 - 34(51.47)^2}{34}} = 14.42$$

---

**EXAMPLE**

**A4** *Calculating Overall Mean and Standard Deviation for Example A3*

| Class | No. of students | Sum marks | Mean | Sum squares | Standard deviation |
|---|---|---|---|---|---|
| 1 | 19 | 923 | 48.6 | 48138 | 13.1 |
| 2 | 15 | 827 | 55.1 | 49006 | 15.2 |
| Total | 34 (= $n_T$) | 1750 (= $\Sigma x_T$) | | 97144 (= $\Sigma x_T{}^2$) | |

## Reliability

The reliability $r$ for a paper of compulsory constructed-answer questions is found from

$$r = \frac{k}{k-1}\left(1 - \frac{\Sigma\sigma_i^2}{\sigma_T^2}\right)$$ where

$k$ is the number of questions,
$\sigma_i$ is the standard deviation of a question,
$\Sigma\sigma_i^2$ is the sum of the squared standard deviations for all questions,
$\sigma_T$ is the standard deviation of marks for the paper as a whole.

In Example A5 there are 10 compulsory questions with individual standard deviations as shown. The standard deviation of marks for the paper as a whole is 11.89. In this example

$$r = \frac{10}{9}\left(1 - \frac{56.61}{11.89^2}\right)$$
$$= 0.67$$

### EXAMPLE

**A5** *Calculation of Reliability*

| Question | $\sigma$ | $\sigma^2$ |
|---|---|---|
| 1 | 2.22 | 4.93 |
| 2 | 1.67 | 2.79 |
| 3 | 2.37 | 5.62 |
| 4 | 1.50 | 2.25 |
| 5 | 2.36 | 5.57 |
| 6 | 2.13 | 4.54 |
| 7 | 2.24 | 5.02 |
| 8 | 2.99 | 8.94 |
| 9 | 3.53 | 12.46 |
| 10 | 2.12 | 4.49 |
| Total | | 56.61 |

# B

# Analysis of Compulsory Questions

It is possible to compile a frequency distribution of marks for the question, using a method similar to that described for the paper as a whole (see Appendix A). From this, the mean and standard deviation of marks can be calculated.

If, however, the choice index and discrimination are to be calculated, it is better to work from a single table which can be used to find mean and standard deviation, choice index and discrimination.

Prepare the table as shown in Example B1. Initially the only columns which can be completed are:

Col.1 student number or name
Col.2 total mark for the paper, $x_T$
Col.4 mark for Question 1, $x_1$
Col.9 mark for Question 2, $x_2$
Columns for marks for subsequent questions

(Note: Column 8 is only required if the longer method of calculating the discrimination is chosen — see note on discrimination on page 179.)

If not already calculated, the question paper mean $M_T$ and standard deviation $\sigma_T$ are found from the table as follows:

$$M_T = \frac{\Sigma x_T}{n_T} \qquad \sigma_T = \sqrt{\frac{\Sigma x_T^2 - n_T M_T^2}{n_T}}$$ where

$\Sigma x_T$ is the sum of marks on the paper as a whole (sum of col. 2 entries),
$n_T$ is the number of students taking the paper,
$\Sigma x_T^2$ is the sum of the squares of marks on the paper as a whole (sum of col. 3 entries).

## EXAMPLE

**B1** *Analysis of Compulsory Questions*

| 1<br>Student | 2<br>Total mark<br>$x_T$ | 3<br>$x_T^2$ | 4<br>Mark for Q1<br>$x_1$ | 5<br>$x_1^2$ | 6<br>$x_{T-1}$ | 7<br>$x_{T-1}^2$ | 8<br>Product<br>$x_1 \, x_{T-1}$ | 9<br>Mark for Q2<br>$x_2$ |
|---|---|---|---|---|---|---|---|---|
| 1 | 95 | 9025 | 9 | 81 | 86 | 7396 | 774 | 9 |
| 2 | 83 | 6888 | 6 | 36 | 77 | 5929 | 462 | 8 |
| 3 | 74 | 5476 | 3 | 9 | 71 | 5041 | 213 | 3 |
| 4 | 70 | 4900 | 10 | 100 | 60 | 3600 | 600 | 8 |
| 5 | 68 | 4624 | 9 | 81 | 59 | 3481 | 531 | 2 |
| 6 | 68 | 4624 | 10 | etc. | 58 | etc. | etc. | 8 |
| 7 | 67 | 4489 | 10 | | 57 | | | 9 |
| 8 | 64 | 4096 | 10 | | 54 | | | 7 |
| 9 | 64 | 4096 | 5 | | 59 | | | 7 |
| 10 | 61 | 3721 | 6 | | 55 | | | 9 |
| 11 | 61 | 3721 | 6 | | 55 | | | 7 |
| 12 | 59 | 3481 | 9 | | 50 | | | 6 |
| 13 | 59 | 3481 | 3 | | 56 | | | 9 |
| 14 | 57 | 3249 | 5 | | 52 | | | 7 |
| 15 | 57 | 3249 | 7 | | 50 | | | 7 |
| 16 | 56 | 3136 | 7 | | 49 | | | 4 |
| 17 | 53 | 2809 | 10 | | 43 | | | 2 |
| 18 | 50 | 2500 | 8 | | 42 | | | 2 |
| 19 | 46 | 2116 | 6 | | 40 | | | 5 |
| 20 | 45 | 2025 | 2 | | 43 | | | 8 |
| 21 | 45 | 2025 | 2 | | 43 | | | 2 |
| 22 | 44 | 1936 | 8 | | 36 | | | 7 |
| 23 | 44 | 1936 | — | | 44 | | | 8 |
| 24 | 43 | 1849 | 7 | | 36 | | | 3 |
| 25 | 41 | 1681 | 4 | | 37 | | | 2 |
| 26 | 41 | 1681 | 3 | | 38 | | | 7 |
| 27 | 41 | 1681 | 5 | | 36 | | | 8 |
| 28 | 38 | 1444 | 4 | | 34 | | | 3 |
| 29 | 37 | 1369 | — | | 37 | | | 9 |
| 30 | 26 | 676 | — | | 26 | | | — |
| Total<br>*n*<br>Mean | 1657<br>30<br>55.23 | 97984 | 174<br>30(27)<br>5.8 (6.44) | 1304 | 1483<br>30<br>49.43 | 78497 | 9092 | |

In Example B1

$$M_T = \frac{1657}{30}$$
$$= 55.23$$
$$\sigma_T = \sqrt{\frac{97984 - 30(55.23)^2}{30}}$$
$$= 14.69$$

For question papers not marked out of 100, the mean and standard deviation can be converted to percentages from the expressions

$$\frac{M_T \times 100}{b_T} \quad \text{and} \quad \frac{\sigma_T \times 100}{b_T}$$

where $b_T$ is the base, the maximum mark obtainable for the paper.

## Choice Index

From the table, the choice index for Question 1, $C_1$, is found from

$$C_1 = \frac{n_1 \times 100}{n_T}$$

where

$n_1$ is the number of students attempting Question 1,
$n_T$ is the total number of students for the paper.

In this case

$$C_1 = \frac{27 \times 100}{30}$$
$$= 90\%$$

## Expected Choice Index

The expected choice index for a compulsory question is 100%.

## Mean Mark for Question

It is normally best to find the 'corrected mean'; this counts students who omitted the question as having scored 0 on the assumption that they omitted it because they were unable, through lack of knowledge, to answer it. The corrected mean, $M_1$, for Question 1 is found from

$$M_1 = \frac{\Sigma x_1}{n_T}$$ where

$\Sigma x_1$ is the sum of marks on Question 1 (from column 4),
$n_T$ is the number of students taking the paper.

In Example B 1

$$M_1 = \frac{174}{30}$$

$$= 5.8$$

This is a 'raw mark'; to convert it to a percentage multiply by $100/b_1$ where $b_1$ is the base, the maximum mark obtainable for the question. In Example B1

$$\text{percentage mean} = \frac{5.8 \times 100}{10}$$

$$= 58.0\%$$

If it is required to find the uncorrected mean, $M_{a1}$ which disregards students who omitted the question, the formula is

$$M_{a1} = \frac{\Sigma x_1}{n_1}$$ where

$\Sigma x_1$ is the sum of marks on Question 1,
$n_1$ is the number of students attempting Question 1.

In Example B1

$$M_{a1} = \frac{174}{27}$$

$$= 6.44$$

## Standard Deviation for Question

The formula given below is for the corrected standard deviation, which treats students who omitted the question as having scored 0. The corrected standard deviation of marks for Question 1, $\sigma_1$, is found from

$$\sigma_1 = \sqrt{\frac{\Sigma x_1^2 - n_T M_1^2}{n_T}}$$ where

$\Sigma x_1^2$ is the sum of squares of marks for Question 1 (column 5),
$M_1$ is the corrected mean for Question 1,
$n_T$ is the number of students taking the paper.

In Example B1

$$\sigma_1 = \sqrt{\frac{1304 - 30(5.8)^2}{30}}$$
$$= 3.135$$

To convert to a percentage, multiply by $100/b_1$ where $b_1$ is the base, the maximum mark obtainable for Question 1. In this case

$$\text{percentage standard deviation} = \frac{3.135 \times 100}{10}$$
$$= 31.35\%$$

## Mean-total for Question

The mean-total for a question is the average mark obtained on the paper as a whole by the students who attempted that question. This is important in an optional question, but not usually significant in a compulsory question. If it is required, the mean-total for Question 1, $M_{T(1)}$, can be found from

$$M_{T(1)} = \frac{\Sigma x_{T(1)}}{n_1}$$ where

$\Sigma x_{T(1)}$ is the sum of scores on the whole paper of students who attempted Question 1,
$n_1$ is the number of students attempting Question 1.

In Example B1, $\Sigma x_{T(1)}$ is 1550. This is equal to the sum of marks of *all* students on the whole paper *minus* the whole-paper marks of those three students who omitted Question 1 (1657 − 44 − 37 − 26). Then

$$M_{T(1)} = \frac{1550}{27}$$

$$= 57.41$$

If necessary, convert to a percentage by multiplying by $100/b_T$ where $b_T$ is the base (maximum mark obtainable) for the paper.

## Facility

No separate calculation of facility is required for a compulsory question, as the corrected mean for the question ($M_1$) will give the necessary indication as to its difficulty.

## Discrimination

The discrimination index of a question is a measure of the correlation between marks on that question and marks on the rest of the paper (which equal total mark for the paper minus the mark for the question under consideration). The stages involved in calculating this discrimination accurately are given below. (For a quick approximate estimation see page 181.)

(*a*) Complete the $x_{T\text{-}1}$ column, (Col. 6), which shows, for each student, mark on the paper minus the mark on Question 1.

(*b*) Find the mean of the $x_{T\text{-}1}$ marks, $M_{T\text{-}1}$, from

$$M_{T\text{-}1} = M_T - M_1$$

where

$M_T$ is the mean for the paper as a whole,
$M_1$ is the corrected mean for Question 1.

In Example B1

$$M_{T\text{-}1} = 55.23 - 5.8$$
$$= 49.43$$

As a *check*, if Column 6 is totalled, to give $\Sigma x_{T\text{-}1}$, then

$$M_{T\text{-}1} = \frac{\Sigma x_{T\text{-}1}}{n_T}$$

In Example B1

$$M_{T\text{-}1} = \frac{1483}{30}$$
$$= 49.43$$

(*c*) Find and total the squares of the $x_{T\text{-}1}$ marks (Col. 7) to give $\Sigma x_{T\text{-}1}{}^2$.

(*d*) Find the standard deviation of the $x_{T-1}$ marks, $\sigma_{T-1}$, from

$$\sigma_{T-1} = \sqrt{\frac{\Sigma x_{T-1}{}^2 - n_T M_{T-1}{}^2}{n_T}}$$ where

$\Sigma x_{T-1}{}^2$ is the sum of squares of the $x_{T-1}$ marks,
$M_{T-1}$ is the mean of the $x_{T-1}$ marks,
$n_T$ is the number of students for the paper.

In Example B1

$$\sigma_{T-1} = \sqrt{\frac{78497 - 30(49.43)^2}{30}}$$
$$= 13.16$$

(*e*) Find the discrimination for Question 1, $D_1$, from

$$D_1 = \frac{\sigma_T{}^2 - \sigma_1{}^2 - \sigma_{T-1}{}^2}{2\,\sigma_1\,\sigma_{T-1}}$$ where

$\sigma_T$ is the standard deviation of marks on the paper as a whole
$\sigma_1$ is the standard deviation of marks on Question 1,
$\sigma_{T-1}$ is the standard deviation of the $x_{T-1}$ marks.

In Example B1

$$D_1 = \frac{14.69^2 - 3.135^2 - 13.16^2}{2 \times 3.135 \times 13.16}$$
$$= 0.40$$

*Note*
It is more usual to describe the calculation of a correlation in terms of the products of the pairs of marks to be correlated; in question discrimination, the product would be, for each student, mark on the question ($x_1$) times $x_{T-1}$ mark (= total mark, minus mark on the question). If this method is to be used, the procedure involves Steps (*a*) to (*d*) as given above, then:

(*e*) Complete and total the ($x_1 x_{T-1}$) product column (Col. 8) to give $\Sigma x_1 x_{T-1}$.

(*f*) Find the discrimination for Question 1, $D_1$, from

$$D_1 = \frac{\Sigma x_1 x_{T-1} - n_T\,M_1\,M_{T-1}}{n_T\,\sigma_1\,\sigma_{T-1}}$$ where

$\Sigma x_1 x_{T-1}$ is the sum of products,
$M_1$ is the mean for Question 1;

$\sigma_1$ is the standard deviation for question 1,
$M_{T-1}$ is the mean of the $x_{T-1}$ marks,
$\sigma_{T-1}$ is the standard deviation of the $x_{T-1}$ marks,
$n_T$ is the number of students for the paper.

In Example B1

$$D_1 = \frac{9092 - 30 \times 5.8 \times 49.43}{30 \times 3.135 \times 13.16}$$
$$= 0.40$$

The first method given is likely to be shorter if a number of questions are being analysed, because the question paper standard deviation can be found once and reused in the calculation of discrimination for each question. In the second method, the product column has to be calculated separately for each question.

## Graphs of Discrimination

The discrimination of a question can be shown graphically instead of by the single figure of the discrimination index, which is tedious to calculate. The steps required are as follows:

(*a*) Divide the students who attempted the question (in the case of a compulsory question, take all students for the paper) into four groups, as nearly as possible equal in size. The top group, or 'upper quartile' contains the students who scored best on the paper as a whole, the second quartile those who scored next best, and so on. If allowed, arrange the scripts in four piles, one for each quartile.

### EXAMPLE

**B2** *Quartile Means for Example B1*

| Quartile | No. of students | Range of scores for the paper | Total scores for Q1 | Mean for Q1 |
|---|---|---|---|---|
| 1 | 7 | 67-95 | 57 | 8.14 |
| 2 | 8 | 57-64 | 51 | 6.38 |
| 3 | 8 | 44-56 | 43 | 5.38 |
| 4 | 7 | 26-43 | 23 | 3.29 |

(*b*) Find the marks on the question under consideration of the students in each quartile and calculate the mean for each quartile.

(*c*) Plot the results graphically.

For Question 1 in Example B1, the stages would be as shown in Example B2 and the resultant graph, as shown in Example B3.

## Estimate of Approximate Discrimination

It is possible to estimate the discrimination from the mean marks obtained on the question by the top and bottom quartiles. However, this is only an approximation, as it takes no account of the marks of the middle two quartiles

**EXAMPLE**

**B3** *Graph of Quartile Means for Example B1*

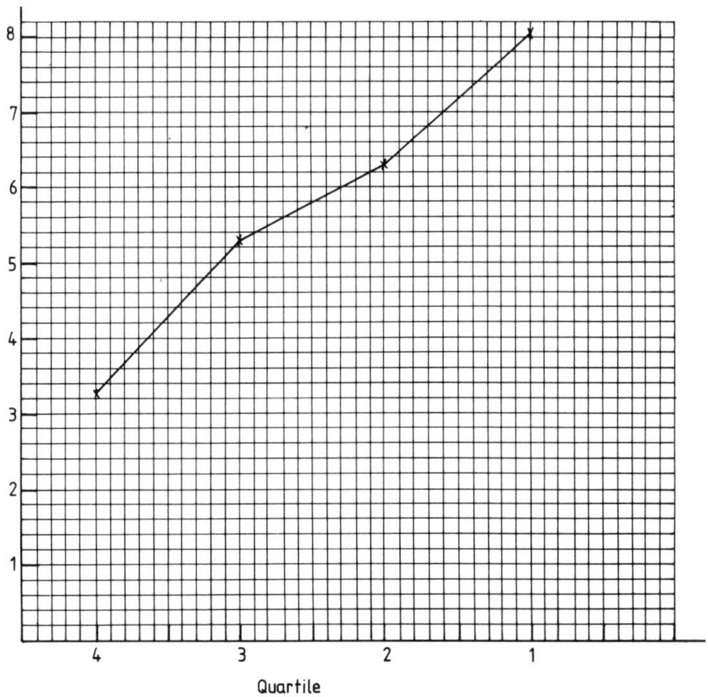

or of the relative positions of students within the top or bottom quartile. The formula for this estimate of the discrimination of Question 1, $D_1$, is:

$$D_1 = \frac{M_{UG} - M_{LG}}{b_1}$$

where

$M_{UG}$ is the mean mark on Question 1 of the students in the top quartile on the test as a whole (the 'Upper Group');

$M_{LG}$ is the mean mark on Question 1 of the students in the bottom quartile on the test as a whole (the 'lower group'),

$b_1$ is the base (maximum mark obtainable) for Question 1.

In Examples B1 and B2,

$$D_1 = \frac{8.14 - 3.29}{10} = 0.49$$

This is higher than the discrimination of 0.40 calculated by either of the longer methods: the estimate obtained by this approximate method may be either high or low.

# C

# Analysis of Optional Questions

It is possible to compile a frequency distribution of the marks for the question using a method similar to that described for the paper as a whole (see Appendix A). From this the mean and standard deviation of marks can be calculated.

If, however, the choice index, facility and discrimination are to be calculated, it is better to work from a table which can be used to give mean and standard deviation, choice index, facility and discrimination.

Prepare the table as shown in Example C1. Initially the only columns which can be completed are:

Col. 1 student number or name
Col. 2 total mark for the paper, $x_T$
Col. 4 mark for Question, 1, $x_1$
Col. 9 mark for Question 2, $x_2$ and columns for other question marks.

(Column 8 is required only if the product method of calculating the discrimination is chosen – see pages 190–191.)

If not already calculated, the mean mark for the paper $M_T$ is found from

$$M_T = \frac{\Sigma x_T}{n_T}$$ where

$\Sigma x_T$ is the sum of marks for the paper as a whole (Column 2),
$n_T$ is the total number of students.

In Example C1

$$M_T = \frac{1421}{30}$$

$$= 47.37$$

If $b_T$ the 'base' or maximum mark obtainable for the paper, is not 100, the mean may be converted to a percentage by multiplying by $100/b_T$.

## EXAMPLE

### C1 *Analysis of Optional Questions*

| 1<br>Student | 2<br>Total mark<br>$x_T$ | 3<br>$x_T^2$ | 4<br>Mark for Q 1<br>$x_1$ | 5<br>$x_1^2$ | 6<br>$x_{T-1}$ | 7<br>$x_{T-1}^2$ | 8<br>Product<br>$x_1 x_{T-1}$ | 9<br>Mark for Q 2<br>$x_2$ etc |
|---|---|---|---|---|---|---|---|---|
| 1 | 39 | 1521 | 3 | 9 | 36 | 1296 | 108 | |
| 2 | 55 | 3025 | 5 | 25 | 50 | 2500 | 250 | |
| 3 | 49 | 2401 | 5 | 25 | 44 | 1936 | 220 | |
| 4 | 37 | 1369 | — | | | | | |
| 5 | 60 | 3600 | 4 | 16 | 56 | 3136 | 224 | |
| 6 | 39 | 1521 | — | etc. | — | — | etc | |
| 7 | 33 | 1089 | 6 | | 27 | | | |
| 8 | 67 | 4489 | 7 | | 60 | | | |
| 9 | 47 | 2209 | 7 | | 40 | | | |
| 10 | 53 | 2809 | — | | | | | |
| 11 | 53 | 2809 | 2 | | 51 | | | |
| 12 | 36 | 1296 | — | | | | | |
| 13 | 26 | 676 | 6 | | 20 | | | |
| 14 | 37 | 1369 | 5 | | 32 | | | |
| 15 | 33 | 1089 | 2 | | 31 | | | |
| 16 | 43 | 1849 | — | | | | | |
| 17 | 38 | 1444 | 4 | | 34 | | | |
| 18 | 48 | 2304 | — | | | | | |
| 19 | 61 | 3721 | 10 | | 51 | | | |
| 20 | 64 | 4096 | 5 | | 59 | | | |
| 21 | 32 | 1024 | 7 | | 25 | | | |
| 22 | 48 | 2304 | 7 | | 41 | | | |
| 23 | 19 | 361 | — | | | | | |
| 24 | 74 | 5476 | — | | | | | |
| 25 | 51 | 2601 | 6 | | 45 | | | |
| 26 | 40 | 1600 | 2 | | 38 | | | |
| 27 | 46 | 2116 | 7 | | 39 | | | |
| 28 | 62 | 3844 | — | | | | | |
| 29 | 75 | 5625 | 10 | | 65 | | | |
| 30 | 56 | 3136 | — | | | | | |
| Total | 1421 | | 110 | 706 | 844 | 38542 | 4780 | |
| $n$ | 30 | | 20 | | 20 | | | |
| Mean | 47.37 | | 5.5 | | 42.2 | | | |
| $\sigma$ | | | | 2.25 | | 12.09 | | |

The standard deviation of marks for the paper as a whole is not needed in the analysis of individual optional questions. If it is to be found at this stage, total the $x_T^2$ column (Column 3).

The standard deviation $\sigma_T$ is then found from

$$\sigma_T = \sqrt{\frac{\Sigma x_T^2 - n_T M_T^2}{n_T}}$$ where

$\Sigma x_T^2$ is the sum of squares of marks for the paper as a whole (column 3),
$M_T$ is the question paper mean,
$n_T$ is the number of students for the paper as a whole

## Choice Index

The choice index for Question 1, $C_1$, is found from

$$C_1 = \frac{n_1 \times 100}{n_T}$$ where

$n_1$ is the number of students attempting Question 1,
$n_T$ is the total number of students taking the paper

In Example C1

$$C_1 = \frac{20 \times 100}{30} = 66.7\%$$

## Expected Choice Index

The expected choice index $EC$ is the choice index which would be obtained if all questions were equally popular and if all students attempted the required number of questions. It is found from the formula

$$EC = \frac{k_a \times 100}{k_T}$$ where

$k_a$ is the number of questions which students are required to attempt,
$k_T$ is the total number of questions from which the selection is made.

For example, in a paper where students are required to attempt five questions out of eight, the expected choice index

$$EC = \frac{5 \times 100}{8} = 62.5\%$$

If there are different requirements for each section of a question paper, then it is necessary to calculate the expected choice index separately for each section. For example, if students are required to attempt all of Questions 1—10 and any three of Questions 11—14.

*EC* for each of Questions 1—10 is 100%

*EC* for each of Questions 11—14 is

$$\frac{3 \times 100}{4} = 75\%$$

## Mean Mark for Question

In a paper offering a choice of questions, the mean mark for a question is, of course, calculated only from the marks of those students who attempted the question. The mean mark for attempts at Question 1, $M_{a1}$, is found from

$$M_{a1} = \frac{\Sigma x_1}{n_1}$$ where

$\Sigma x_1$ is the sum of marks obtained for Question 1 (Col. 4),
$n_1$ is the number of students attempting Question 1.

In Example C1

$$M_{a1} = \frac{110}{20} = 5.50$$

To convert to a percentage, multiply by $100/b_1$ where $b_1$ is the base, the maximum mark obtainable for Question 1. In this case percentage mean

$$= \frac{5.50 \times 100}{10} = 55.0\%$$

## Standard Deviation for the Question

The standard deviation of marks for attempts at Question 1, $\sigma_{a1}$ is found from

$$\sigma_{a1} = \sqrt{\frac{\Sigma x_1^2 - n_1 M_{a1}^2}{n_1}}$$ where

$\Sigma x_1^2$ is the sum of squares of marks for Question 1 (Col. 5),
$M_{a1}$ is the mean mark for Question 1,
$n_1$ is the number of students attempting Question 1.

In Example C1

$$\sigma_{a1} = \sqrt{\frac{706 - 20\,(5.5)^2}{20}}$$
$$= 2.25$$

As a percentage $\sigma_{a1} = \dfrac{2.25 \times 100}{b_1} = \dfrac{2.25 \times 100}{10} = 22.5\%$

## Mean-total

The mean-total mark for a question is the mean mark obtained on the paper as a whole by those students who attempted the question under consideration. To find the mean-total for Question 1, first identify (from Col. 2) the $x_T$ marks, i.e. total marks for the paper, of *only* those students who attempted Question 1. Add these marks to give $\Sigma x_{T(1)}$. In Example C1 the total is 954.

The mean-total for Question 1, $M_{T(1)}$ is then found from

$$M_{T(1)} = \frac{\Sigma x_{T(1)}}{n_1}$$ where

$\Sigma x_{T(1)}$ is the sum of marks on the paper as a whole of those students who attempted Question 1,
$n_1$ is the number of students attempting Question 1.

In Example C1

$$M_{T(1)} = \frac{954}{20}$$
$$= 47.70$$

The mean-total is converted to a percentage, if necessary, by multiplying by $100/b_T$ where $b_T$ is the base, the maximum mark obtainable for the paper as a whole.

(*Note.* If the proportion of students who omitted the question is small, it will be quicker to find $\Sigma x_{T(1)}$ by adding the marks on the paper as a whole of those students who did *not* attempt Question 1 and subtracting the answer from $\Sigma x_T$ the sum of the marks of *all* students for the paper as a whole.)

## Facility

The facility of a question is an estimate of the percentage mean mark which would have been obtained on the question if it had been attempted by students whose average ability was the same as that of all the students for the paper. The facility* for Question 1, $F_1$ is found from

$$F_1 = M_{a1} + M_T - M_{T(1)}$$

where

$M_{a1}$ is the mean mark for Question 1 expressed as a percentage,
$M_T$ is the mean for the paper as a whole, expressed as a percentage, and
$M_{T(1)}$ is the mean-total for Question 1, expressed as a percentage.

In Example C1

$$F_1 = 55.0 + 47.37 - 47.7 = 54.67\%$$

## Discrimination

The discrimination index for a question is a measure of the correlation between marks on that question and marks on the rest of the paper (which

---

*In *British Examinations: Techniques of Analysis* (Slough, NFER, 1972) Dr R. B. Morrison, who has been responsible for much of the pioneer work on the analysis of non-objective questions, suggests a different formula for facility. Expressed in the notation we have been using, this formula is

$$F_1 = M_{a1} + 50 - M_{T(1)}$$

$M_{a1}$ is the mean mark for Question 1 expressed as a percentage and
$M_{T(1)}$ is the mean-total for Question 1 expressed as a percentage.

In Example C1

$$F = 55 + 50 - 47.7 = 57.3\%$$

This formula is based on the assumption that the average student, marked by a marker of average severity, will score 50% on the paper as a whole. The claimed advantage of this facility is that (unlike the facility of objective questions) it does not vary with the ability of the students taking the paper as a whole. The disadvantage is that it does vary with the difficulty of the paper in which the question is included; it may give quite a false impression of the ease or difficulty of the question if the mean mark for the paper as a whole differs greatly from 50%.

equal total mark for the paper minus mark for the question under consideration). The stages involved in calculating the discrimination of an optional question are as follows:

(*a*) Complete the $x_{T\text{-}1}$ column (Col. 6) which shows, for each student attempting question 1, the mark for the paper as a whole minus the mark for Question 1.

(*b*) Find $M_{T\text{-}1}$ the mean of the $x_{T\text{-}1}$ marks from

$$M_{T\text{-}1} = M_{T(1)} - M_{a1} \quad \text{where}$$

$M_{T(1)}$ is the mean-total for Question 1,
$M_{a1}$ is the mean mark for Question 1.

In Example C1, $M_{T\text{-}1} = 47.70 - 5.5$
$= 42.20$

As a *check*, if column 6 is totalled to give $\Sigma x_{T\text{-}1}$, then

$$M_{T\text{-}1} = \frac{\Sigma x_{T\text{-}1}}{n_1}$$

In Example 20.1

$$M_{T\text{-}1} = \frac{844}{20} = 42.20$$

(*c*) Complete the $x_{T\text{-}1}{}^2$ column (Col. 7) which gives the squares of the $x_{T\text{-}1}$ marks and add these squares to give $\Sigma x_{T\text{-}1}{}^2$

(*d*) Find the standard deviation of the $x_{T\text{-}1}$ marks, $\sigma_{T\text{-}1}$, from

$$\sigma_{T\text{-}1} = \sqrt{\frac{\Sigma x_{T\text{-}1}{}^2 - n_1 M_{T\text{-}1}{}^2}{n_1}} \quad \text{where}$$

$\Sigma x_{T\text{-}1}{}^2$ is the sum of squares of the $x_{T\text{-}1}$ marks,
$M_{T\text{-}1}$ is the mean of the $x_{T\text{-}1}$ marks,
$n_1$ is the number of students attempting Question 1.

In Example C1

$$\sigma_{T\text{-}1} = \sqrt{\frac{38542 - 20(42.2)^2}{20}} = 12.09$$

then **EITHER**

(*e*) (i) Identify (from Col. 3) the $x_T{}^2$ marks (the squares of marks on the paper as a whole) of *only* those students who attempted Question 1. Add them to give $\Sigma x_{T(1)}{}^2$

(*f*) (i) Find $\sigma_{T(1)}$ the standard deviation of marks on the paper as a whole of those students who attempted Question 1, from

$$\sigma_{T(1)} = \sqrt{\frac{\Sigma x_{T(1)}{}^2 - n_1 M_{T(1)}{}^2}{n_1}}$$ where

$\Sigma x_{T(1)}{}^2$ is the sum of squares of marks on the paper as a whole for students attempting Question 1,
$M_{T(1)}$ is the mean of marks on the paper as a whole for students attempting Question 1 (mean-total),
$n_1$ is the number of students attempting Question 1.

In Example C1

$$\sigma_{T(1)} = \sqrt{\frac{48808 - 20\,(47.7)^2}{20}}$$
$$= 12.85$$

(*g*) (i) Find $D_1$ the discrimination for Question 1, from

$$D_1 = \frac{\sigma_{T(1)}{}^2 - \sigma_{a1}{}^2 - \sigma_{T\text{-}1}{}^2}{2\,\sigma_{a1}\,\sigma_{T\text{-}1}}$$ where

$\sigma_{T(1)}$ is the standard deviation of marks on the whole paper of students attempting Question 1,
$\sigma_{a1}$ is the standard deviation of marks on Question 1,
$\sigma_{T\text{-}1}$ is the standard deviation of $x_{T\text{-}1}$ marks.

In Example C1

$$D_1 = \frac{12.85^2 - 2.25^2 - 12.09^2}{2 \times 2.25 \times 12.09}$$
$$= 0.26$$

**OR**

(*e*) (ii) complete the product column (Col. 8) by multiplying the marks on the question ($x_1$, Col. 4) by the $x_{T\text{-}1}$ mark (Col. 6) and add the column to give $\Sigma x_1\, x_{T\text{-}1}$.

(*f*) (ii) find the discrimination for Question 1, $D_1$, from

$$D_1 = \frac{\Sigma x_1\, x_{T\text{-}1} - n_1\, M_{a1}\, M_{T\text{-}1}}{n_1\, \sigma_{a1}\, \sigma_{T\text{-}1}}$$ where

$\Sigma x_1 x_{T-1}$ is the sum of the products of $x_1$ and $x_{T-1}$ (Col. 8),
$M_{a1}$ is the mean mark for Question 1,
$\sigma_{a1}$ is the standard deviation of marks for Question 1,
$M_{T-1}$ is the mean of the $x_{T-1}$ marks,
$\sigma_{T-1}$ is the standard deviation of the $x_{T-1}$ marks.
$n_1$ is the number of students attempting Question 1.

In Example C1

$$D_1 = \frac{4780 - 20 \times 5.5 \times 42.2}{20 \times 2.25 \times 12.09}$$

$$= 0.25$$

(*Note.* If the standard deviations are calculated to 4 decimal places the discrimination is 0.2539 by either method.)

The first method is likely to prove the quicker, as the $x_T{}^2$ values can be read from Column 3 each time they are needed, whereas the product for each student must be found separately for each question analysed. Also, a pre-programmed calculator can be used to find the standard deviations required.

See Appendix B for the preparation of graphs of discrimination and the estimate of approximate discrimination.

# D

# Predicting the Mean and Standard Deviation for a Compiled Paper of Compulsory Questions

The following method may be used to predict in advance what will be the mean mark and standard deviation of a question paper which contains only compulsory questions and has been compiled from banked questions for which the previous analysis is known.

## Question Paper Mean

The mean mark $M_T$ for the paper is found from the formula

$$M_T = \Sigma M_i$$ where

$M_i$ is the mean mark for a question,
$\Sigma M_i$ is the sum of means of all questions.

In each case the mean mark is 'raw', not percentage, and the question means are corrected for 'omits', i.e. students who omitted to answer the question are counted as having scored 0.

## Question Paper Standard Deviation

$$\sigma_T = \Sigma \sigma_i D_i$$ where

$\sigma_i$ is the standard deviation of a question
$D_i$ is the discrimination of that question
$\Sigma \sigma_i D_i$ is the sum of products (standard deviation × discrimination)

In each case the mark is 'raw' not percentage.

Example D1 shows the calculation of the predicted mean and standard deviation for a paper of ten questions each marked out of 10, giving a question paper total of 100.

## EXAMPLE

**D1** *Predicted Mean and Standard Deviation*

| Question | Mean | $\sigma$ | Discrimination | $\sigma$D |
|---|---|---|---|---|
| 1 | 5.66 | 2.22 | 0.74 | 1.64 |
| 2 | 5.14 | 1.67 | 0.46 | 0.77 |
| 3 | 4.89 | 2.37 | 0.42 | 1.00 |
| 4 | 6.14 | 1.50 | 0.35 | 0.53 |
| 5 | 3.86 | 2.36 | 0.27 | 0.64 |
| 6 | 2.84 | 2.13 | 0.29 | 0.62 |
| 7 | 6.32 | 2.24 | 0.62 | 1.39 |
| 8 | 2.82 | 2.99 | 0.68 | 2.03 |
| 9 | 2.68 | 3.53 | 0.68 | 2.40 |
| 10 | 4.39 | 2.12 | 0.41 | 0.87 |
| Total | 44.74 | | | 11.89 |

Question paper mean = 44.74
Question paper standard deviation = 11.89

# E

# Predicting the Mean for a Compiled Paper of Optional Questions

The following method of predicting the mean mark for a paper of optional questions compiled from a bank, can only be used if the mean marks of the questions (as shown by previous analysis) are almost exactly the same. If this is the case, then the question paper mean $M_T$ is found from

$$M_T = k_a \, M_{a1}$$

where

$k_a$ is the number of questions to be answered,
$M_{a1}$ is the mean mark (raw, not percentage) of Question 1.

This method does not make any allowance for failure by some students to answer the required number of questions; the question paper mean would, of course, be reduced if there were any significant under-answering. This is something which is difficult to predict in advance, except by noting the pattern of answers in past papers; even that may not be a reliable guide.

# F

# Statistical Notation Used in the Book

Throughout the book, whenever a formula is given, the symbols used are defined. For convenience, however, the meanings of all the symbols used in the book are given in this Appendix.

$b$ base, the maximum mark obtainable

- $b_1$ base for Question 1
- $b_2$ base for Question 2
- $b_T$ base for the whole paper

$C$ choice index

- $C_1$ choice index for Question 1
- $C_2$ choice index for Question 2

$D$ discrimination

- $D_1$ discrimination of Question 1
- $D_2$ discrimination of Question 2
- $D_i$ discrimination of a question

$EC$ expected choice index

$F$ facility

$f$ frequency (the number of students with a given mark)

$k$ number of questions

- $k_a$ number of questions to be attempted
- $k_T$ number of questions in the paper

$M$ mean

- $M_1$ mean for Question 1 (this is the 'corrected mean', counting students who omitted the question as having scored 0)
- $M_2$ mean for Question 2 (corrected)
- $M_{a1}$ the uncorrected mean for Question 1, based only on the marks of those students who attempted it

- $M_{a2}$ the uncorrected mean for Question 2
- $M_i$ mean for a question
- $M_T$ the mean for the whole paper (all students)
- $M_{T(1)}$ the 'mean-total' for Question 1, i.e. the mean obtained on the whole paper by those students who attempted Question 1
- $M_{T-1}$ the mean of the (whole paper minus Question 1) marks of the students under consideration

$n$ number of students

- $n_1$ number of students attempting Question 1
- $n_2$ number of students attempting Question 2
- $n_T$ number of students for the whole paper.

$r$ reliability

$x$ a mark

- $x_1$ the mark of any one student on Question 1
- $x_2$ the mark of any one student on Question 2
- $x_T$ the mark of any one student for the whole paper
- $x_{T-1}$ the mark of any one student for (whole paper minus Question 1)

$\sigma$ standard deviation

- $\sigma_1$ corrected standard deviation for Question 1 (the corrected standard deviation counts students who omitted the question as having scored 0)
- $\sigma_2$ corrected standard deviation for Question 2
- $\sigma_{a1}$ uncorrected standard deviation for Question 1 (i.e. based only on those students who attempted the question)
- $\sigma_{a2}$ uncorrected standard deviation for Question 2
- $\sigma_T$ standard deviation for the whole paper
- $\sigma_{T-1}$ standard deviation of (whole paper minus Question 1) marks
- $\sigma_{T(1)}$ standard deviation of marks for the whole paper of only those students who attempted Question 1
- $\sigma_i$ standard deviation of a question

$\Sigma$ sum of

- $\Sigma x_1$ the sum of marks on Question 1
- $\Sigma x_T$ the sum of marks on the whole paper

# Further Reading


Bloom, B.S. (ed.) *Taxonomy of Educational Objectives: the Classification of Education Goals. Handbook I: Cognitive Domain* (London: Longmans, 1956)

*Council of Technical Examining Bodies, SI Symbols, Abbreviations and Conventions* (City & Guilds of London Institute, 2nd edn 1976)

Ebel, R.L. *Essentials of Educational Measurement* (Englewood Cliffs, New Jersey: Prentice-Hall, 1972)

Gronlund N.E. *Stating Behavioural Objectives for Classroom Instruction* (London: Macmillan, 1970)

Gronlund, N.E. *Constructing Achievement Tests* (Englewood Cliffs, New Jersey: Prentice-Hall, 1968)

Hudson, B. (ed.) *Assessment Techniques: an Introduction.* (London: Methuen, 1973)

Macintosh, H.G. *Techniques and Problems of Assessment: a Practical Handbook for Teachers* (London: Edward Arnold, 1974)

Nuttall, D.S. and Wilmott, A.S. *British Examinations: Techniques of Analysis* (Slough: NFER, 1972)

# Index